The Merger Game

The Merger Game

STAN SAUERHAFT

DRAWINGS BY Jack Fuller

THOMAS Y. CROWELL COMPANY
New York   Established 1834

Except for a few passing references to obvious historical people and companies, all characters and companies in this book are composites and creations of the imagination. They are intended to illustrate certain aspects of life in our contemporary business world and not to report the conduct of real people or organizations. Thus, any resemblance to persons living or dead is coincidental.
Portions of this book originally appeared in *Dun's Review*.

Manufactured in the United States of America

Library of Congress Catalog Card Number: 70-146288
ISBN 0-690-53213-X

1   2   3   4   5   6   7   8   9   10

FOR Ro, Rich, Doug, and Rob—
whose unflagging interest I could never arouse

Preface

IT WAS A PHENOMENON THAT BLOSSOMED RAPIDLY IN THE late 1960's. The merger game. And the protagonist was a new breed of business swashbuckler: the conglomerator. Paralleling his rise was an inordinate increase in the number of heart seizures and gastrointestinal upsets in boardrooms around the country.

Yes it was a time of great danger and high excitement in the financial canyons of the nation. No one was safe, and certainly nothing was sacred. Fortunes were pirated virtually overnight, while some old respected companies went to the bottom and others fought desperately to remain afloat.

But the game was carried too far. Countervailing forces, spurred mostly by fear and a sense of fairness, built up enough pressure on the federal government to slow down this trend to internecine turmoil. Congress began discussing restrictive legislation, and a new Justice Department Antitrust Division administration rolled out powerful legal weapons against some of the leading conglomerators, especially those who had committed the heinous crime of reaching to the very top of the business establishment to pick their plums.

Then an even more potent force took over to really slow down these business aggrandizers: the federal government's decision to severely tighten money in order to fight inflation. This end-of-the-decade policy plunged stocks into the worst bear market since the 1930's, hitting hardest the very conglomerates whose heavy debt-structures had enabled them to do so much swinging. Thus, the number of forcible take-overs and loveless corporate marriages dropped sharply.

Yet as 1970 came to a close, money began to ease, the stock market started to show signs of resuming its more usual upward path, and the denizens of the business jungle began to wonder aloud if the Justice Department might have overreacted against some of the conglomerates. Once again, the conglomerators started to compile lists of potential victims. Some of the same old hands at the game began dusting off some of the same old tricks, with perhaps a few new refinements and combinations. Take-over action started to increase. The rate of bicarbonate consumption around the mahogany conference tables was on the way up again.

This time, the game was not limited to the customary conglomerators. Some rather depressed companies found that they too could play—provided they could find target companies that were still more depressed than themselves, or companies whose stock had not bounced back as well as theirs.

Also, there appeared on the scene still other new grabbers to vie with the old power brokers for the prizes. Some of these new entries, such as money-lending institutions, came cloaked in the utmost respectability. Their methods compare with those of the brazen young conglomerators as the FBI compares with a Western frontier marshal.

So once again the level of excitement is rising down at Broad and Wall, and on Wilshire, State, Montgomery, Peachtree, and LaSalle. It is said that a war is only as good as the people in it. Here is a look behind the scenes at some of the key people and their special styles in the kind of business wars whose results you read about in your daily newspaper. Regardless of how good or how bad you think they are, it is well to know who they are and how they operate. At this moment, the company you work for may be on one of their lists.

Contents

1 / A Handy Guide to the Corporate Raiders

A FORM OF BIG GAME HUNTING IS THE WAY A DISTINGUISHED U. S. senator once described it on the floor of the Senate. And now this company, which is neither one of the really hopeless money-losers in American industry nor a super giant such as AT&T, IBM, or General Motors—the only two types of companies that have been safe in recent years —suddenly discovers it has become somebody's target.

Middling Manufacturing Company is under attack, and the chief gunslinger is about to walk into its boardroom for the first showdown. Middling's management is about to come face to face with the man behind the six-shooter.

What sort of desperado can they expect to confront them?

To their surprise he might be as smooth-talking and impeccably mannered as S. Morgan Farnsworth. Since leaving that noted West Coast conglomerate, Farnsworth has methodically gathered around him several very diverse companies with only his highly refined greed as their common denominator. A graduate of Stanford Business School, he also has degrees in engineering and accounting. As a management consultant for many years with one of the big national firms, he had an opportunity to look at scores of companies from the inside out. Middling may have been one of them. Farnsworth is tall, handsome, articulate—and very tough-minded. He specializes in squeezing excess assets and personnel out of a company once he takes it over.

He is hated in dozens of towns around the country because he closed the old mill or processing plant and threw hundreds of families on relief.

But Farnsworth does not consider that his responsibility. "A business must at least make a fair profit for its owners," he likes to say—although his idea of a fair profit has been questioned on occasion. "Fair," he says, "is better than mediocre, but much less than great. Great is how it is after I've had it for a while." Farnsworth is also a believer in cost cutting. "There isn't a plant in the country," he brags, "where I can't walk in and slash 10 percent off their costs the first year with no drop in production."

As for personnel changes, he will say, of course, that none will be made unless they are mutually agreed upon. However, he will add that such changes are probably easier for him to make since he has no emotional involvement, and he does not mind playing the role of ogre when it is necessary.

For all his urbanity, Farnsworth can get violently angry and is given to table-pounding and high-pitched screaming when opposed by the corporate management of his takeover target. On one occasion, he threatened to take the company by force and broke a chair as he rose to leave a hostile boardroom. To this threat, one of the officers of the embattled company retorted: "You just go ahead, sir, but before you get back here again we will blow up every one of our plants." History records that one as a stalemate.

Quite different from Farnsworth's style is the approach of Plato Archos. Born in Greece, where he was an economics prodigy, Archos fled the country with his family when his father was discovered to be an embezzler, grew up in Switzerland, and finished his education in the United States. He is short and rather stout, has a heavy southern European accent, and wears thick glasses. But he moves quickly and agilely, and is reputed to have been a good soccer player in his youth. Archos is self-conscious about his background, his appearance, and his manner. He has tried to Americanize his image by including national sports heroes on the boards of several of his companies, and he frequents such well-known Manhattan restaurants as Toots Shor's and Twenty One. He does not belong to the Recess Club. Archos will speak very softly on first encounter—almost in a whisper. He will have two lawyers with him, but neither will say a word. His victims are usually awestruck by the intricacy of planning that has gone into his intended takeover. He will seem to know more about their company—their people, products, plants, prospects, and plans—than they do.

The exchange offer for their company's stock that Archos has worked out will seem at first glance to be almost irresistibly attractive. The additional offer to top management executives personally will seem even more alluring. They will realize that he does truly want to work with them. He wants to be accepted in the "right" circles among "nice"

people and is willing to pay a lot for that. Only their personal revulsion will, in the end, stand in the way of the deal. That is Archos' major flaw. He disgusts people.

T. T. (Timmie) Slade is another kettle of fish altogether. One of the fastest moving of all the new conglomerators, Slade rose from the humblest of beginnings in a small town in Arkansas. He says he was an orphan, and nobody can dispute it for he seems to have buried the records of his parents. After finishing six grades of school, Slade knocked around the Southwest and South for a while, got into the auto parts business in Atlanta, and then branched out with his own chain of machine shops. A local banker decided Slade had what it takes to make it big, and began financing him. One of the first things Slade took as he made it big was the banker's own bank, where he installed himself as chief executive. He first achieved national prominence when he fought a sensational proxy fight against a big, old-line lumber company. After Slade won, the head of the company committed suicide.

Before he was forty Slade had been married and divorced three times. His current wife, an ex-Miss Mississippi, can whistle Khachaturian's "Sabre Dance" while pedaling a bicycle uphill with no hands. Slade is very proud of her and has built for her the biggest house in the Southeast.

A master in the art of public relations, Slade has a way of making his intended victim look like the villain, with himself as the shining white knight protecting the interests of stockholders, employees, and community alike. When his eyes light on a company, he may well come around to its headquarters city several weeks before the die is cast. He will be photographed with leading local businessmen on the golf courses and in the finest restaurants, and will make statements about the great future of the city while in the company of local politicians. He will even get his well-known publisher friends up from the South to pass the word along to the local press about what a good corporate citizen Timmie Slade is, and how any community is lucky when he moves in because he allows local management to stay on, increases the number of jobs in town, and contributes to all community good works.

When he finally makes his approach to his target's top management, Slade may very well bring along the president of his most recently acquired company to testify to the fact that working with Timmie Slade is the most profitable and soul-satisfying thing that ever happened to him. Slade's ultimate offer will include handsome salary increases and bonus arrangements for all the company's top management, and the exchange offer for the company's stock will probably include cash, debentures, and warrants. In his twangy, semiliterate speaking style, Slade will present one of the most intricate financial deals that a stunned management has ever come across. They will then realize that they are in the hands of a shrewd professional who is playing several leagues higher than any ball game they have ever been involved in.

If Middling should fall into the widening web of Randolf Blanke, on the other hand, its executives will never see him. His agents will visit them. It is said that the presidents of some of his companies have been hired and years later fired by him without ever having met him. Indeed, it is several years since any living man is known to have seen Blanke, but his presence is felt in many circles.

Blanke's material wealth and holdings are legendary. From an inheritance of $4 million, which he received thirty years ago on graduating from Yale, he has built a half-billion-dollar fortune through shrewd speculations and real-estate maneuverings. On his fiftieth birthday, Blanke reputedly tried to purchase his alma mater outright; he planned to move it to Los Angeles to give the West Coast its first Ivy League college. When last heard to speak, Blanke was reported to be stuttering badly. Besides this impediment, he is very short and has a large mole on his left cheek. Perhaps because he realizes he is physically unattractive, he has never married. More likely, though, he could not stand the thought of sharing his money with anyone else.

If Middling has been chosen to be Blanke's latest trophy, its best weapon in fighting him is to somehow get him into court to answer a lawsuit. Public attention is anathema to him, for it could force him to alter his secretive personal habits, something he spends millions to preserve. However, devising a legal maneuver to get him into court may take a very shrewd and creative law firm—and chances are that most of the best firms are already on retainer to Blanke.

These men—Farnsworth, Archos, Slade, and Blanke —are typical of the raiders that have been preying on companies in recent years. So, unpleasant as the prospect seems, chances are that a company like Middling will be unlucky enough to come up against one of them sooner or later. What hope does it have of beating him off? Its chances of beating off the raid will depend in great part on the degree of experience and shrewdness of the raider. In addition, his financial resources and his general reputation as well as that of his company will have important bearing on the outcome of Middling's fight for survival.

Middling starts with the odds about 3 to 1 in its favor. The two major factors going for it are stockholder inertia and the general antagonism of the business community toward raiders. The odds then shift toward the raider, depending on his moves. For example:

If the raider has accumulated a major position in the company's stock and has become its largest single stockholder, the odds on its beating him off drop to 2 to 1. Many of Middling's potential friendly merger partners will melt away in fear that they would inherit the raider as a huge stockholder in their business if they merged with it— or, indeed, might even be in danger of takeover themselves.

If he makes a cash or exchange offer at least 25 percent above the equivalent of Middling's current stock price and asks for a majority of its stock on a first-come, first-served basis, rather than pro rata, the raider will help to stampede many stockholders and drop Middling's odds to, say, 8 to 5.

If he shrewdly offers to buy any and all shares tendered, not just a majority, then Middling is, at best, even money to survive. He will have most of the arbitragers turning their considerable buying power into his camp. They will be buying Middling's stock up to approximately 10 percent of the exchange value, expecting to turn it in to the raider for full value within a few weeks. For example, if Middling's stock is selling at around $36 and the raider is offering $50 principal amount or subordinated convertible debentures, the arbitragers will probably buy heavily up to $45 and perhaps even higher as the closing day of the tender offer approaches and it appears that the offer will be successful.

(One of the more exciting little spectator sports played on Wall Street is known as "skin the vulture"; that is, catching the arbitrager holding the bag in a long position in a deal that falls through, with resultant plummeting of the stock he holds. When that happens, knowing bystanders quietly applaud. But it rarely happens. The arbitragers are among the shrewdest birds on the Street and, by the size of their combined buying power, can in themselves often be instrumental in putting a deal over.)

Then if the raider has figured out a tax-free exchange

offer so that stockholders can keep all their paper profits without paying immediate taxes, the odds shift against the company, say, to 5 to 7. This may also intrigue the per-formance—or go-go—mutual funds, and their entrance into the market will suck up Middling's stock like a vacuum cleaner. In a matter of a few weeks, thousands of stockhold-ers will disappear from its lists, to be replaced by a few fictional Street names holding hundreds of thousands of shares of Middling's stock. Middling's corporate life is now ebbing fast. These major new stockholders would sell out to the devil for a few points on the upside. They will always go to the sweetest deal, and that favors the raider.

If the raider has set up his deal with one or two of the top investment banking houses as dealer-managers, the odds against the target drop still further—5 to 9. These bankers will use their extensive contacts all over the country and send troops into every big city where Middling has con-centrations of stockholders to get in touch personally with the company's largest holders and explain the advantages of the tender offer. If the raider offers an unusually juicy com-mission that the dealer-managers can parcel out to brokers for each share of the stock they can dig up and turn in, Middling is that much deeper in trouble.

Finally, a lot depends on the law firm, public relations outfit, and proxy-soliciting firm enlisted by the raider. There are only a few really clever and experienced firms in each of these fields (that is, law firms with good contacts at the Securities and Exchange Commission and the ability to move quickly; public relations firms that know all of the ways of reaching stockholders and the investment commu-nity at just the right time—and with the right message; and soliciting firms with good sensitive people in the field), and if the raider has retained them, or at least neutralized them so that the target cannot retain them, then the odds against the company become 1 to 2.

A grim picture it is, with all those factors arrayed against the company. It is made no less grim when one considers what Middling could be faced with if it succeeds in staving off the raider. Middling might have to make a marriage of necessity with another company that it will have to go to bed with each night for the rest of its life. It might have to quickly buy an overlapping-interest company in order to encourage the Justice Department or Federal Trade Commission to step in and disapprove the raid as a potential restraint of trade in one of the raider's main lines of business, although it knows the company will lose a sackful of money for Middling while it owns it.

Middling might be faced with the raider and some of his cohorts holding a substantial minority interest and demanding several seats on its board, if not immediate control. It might begin experiencing a wave of executive resignations from the company by men who are afraid their business careers are in danger of being bogged down in nonproductive, noncreative maneuverings merely to remain in some control of their destinies.

Middling might find some of its biggest industrial customers beginning to shun it because they cannot be sure how long the company will continue to beat off attackers. Rather than wonder what would happen to their source of supply should Middling eventually lose, these old customers decide to start developing alternate sources of supply for the same products that Middling has always furnished.

At this point, as the shades of darkness seem to be inevitably closing down on Middling's future, it surely goes without saying that in one way or another, should a company be singled out as the object of some raider's affection, its management executives' business careers will be irrevocably altered. However, the company may be forced into a new life through a merger with a company even better than itself, or its slow-moving board may be forced into approving that long-pending acquisition which can pump new vitality into the corporate bloodstream. In any case, never sell Pollyanna short. It is one of the most durable commodities around.

2 / The Anatomy of a Raid

THERE HAD BEEN MORE FIRMNESS IN THE PRICE OF TARGET Company's stock for the last several weeks than the financial reports and earnings prospects seemed to warrant. In addition, the trading volume had been two or three times higher than usual. At first Target's top executives were pleased at this indication of interest in their company, but soon it began to trouble them.

Then one morning Frank Pigeon, president of Target, got a telephone call from Ephraim Rader, the noted conglomerator, asking for an urgent appointment the next day. That next day turned out to be a black one. Rader informed Pigeon that he had accumulated 790,000 shares of his company's common stock for "investment purposes," which was 9.9 percent of the 8,000,000 shares outstanding. Rader's company, which made paper cartons, ran an auto rental agency, packed meat, and was the foremost manufacturer of Little League uniforms, was now Target's biggest single stockholder by far, even though Rader's company's total assets were only one-sixth those of Pigeon's company's. By holding just under 10 percent of Target Company's stock, Rader's company was able to avoid falling under the purview of the "insider's" rule, which requires special registration with the Securities and Exchange Commission of all stockholders owning 10 percent or more of a company's shares. Registration strips away the cloak of secrecy, and restrictions on stock trading profits can be imposed.

Now Rader tells Pigeon and the other executives of Target what he plans to do, preferably with their approval, if not enthusiasm. On the following Monday, Rader's law firm will register with the SEC a prospectus detailing an offer for each share of Target Company's stock of $50 principal subordinated convertible debentures which will pay 7 percent interest. They will be convertible at any time on a share-for-share basis into Rader's company's stock, which is currently selling at 49. Furthermore, one-eighth of a warrant to purchase Rader's company's stock at 55 will be issued for a seven-year period. This whole package will be offered to their company stockholders on a one-for-one basis for any and all stock outstanding.

Target Company's stock is now selling at 38, so the potential attractiveness of Rader's offer is immediately apparent. Furthermore, Target pays $2.10 a share in annual dividends, while Rader's convertible debenture would pay the equivalent of $3.50. To this must be added the value of the premium for the conversion right and the market value of the warrants, which would undoubtedly have a public market as soon as they were issued.

While the officers of Target sit in shocked silence contemplating Rader's lightning thrust, Rader mellifluously intones soothing words: to wit, no change in management is contemplated when he takes over; he will not move the business headquarters away from its current site; he has a great deal of respect for the history and reputation of Target Company and does not want to do anything to injure that. However, he sees a few spots where an outsider could add a little creative planning. He wants above all for everything to go smoothly and correctly, but he is prepared for any eventuality.

Two hours after Rader leaves his victims' office, a press release emanates from Rader's company announcing its designs on the firm. A few minutes later the Dow Jones broad tape carries the news, and pandemonium breaks out

around the company's trading post on the floor of the New York Stock Exchange. A torrential influx of "buy" orders forces the Exchange to stop trading in the company's stock. It reopens forty minutes later, up 5 points on a block of 70,000 shares. Some 130,000 shares are traded by 3:30 P.M., more than twenty-five times the normal daily volume, and the stock closes at 44, up 6 points on the day. In the next ten days almost 2,000,000 shares of Target stock, approximately one-quarter of all the shares outstanding, are traded. Almost every day the stock makes the ten-most-active list, usually near the top.

After Target's management tires of moaning "Why us? Why us?" they turn to analyzing just how Rader could afford to offer such a fantastically attractive price for their company. And they discover that Rader is going to do it with the unwitting, though effective, help of the government.

This is how it will work. On the $2.10 per share in dividends that Rader will be receiving on his 790,000 shares of the company's stock, he will pay around 15 cents per share in taxes after taking into account the intercompany tax regulation of Internal Revenue, which excludes 85 percent of dividends from taxation, and the corporate tax rate on the remainder. (An ordinary private stockholder, of course, would have to pay taxes on the dividends at a much higher rate.) This will net him $1.95. Meanwhile, of the $3.50 in debenture interest he will pay out in exchange for each share of Target Company's stock, half will be a write-off against business expenses. Thus, it will really cost him only $1.75. Therefore, he stands to net 20 cents on each share exchanged.

In addition to this immediate monetary bonus, Rader's group will benefit most by getting its hands on the company's assets. This would be accomplished in exchange for mere IOU's, which is all the subordinated debentures really are since they are not backed up by specific assets. As the whipped cream on the package, Rader's company offers one-eighth of a warrant to buy its stock at an inflated price. This actually benefits rather than costs Rader's company, because although the tendering stockholder gets a piece of paper that seemingly has value, he must put additional money into Rader's company treasury should he exercise the warrant. Yet this seeming bonus helps to complete the seduction.

Realization that they have perhaps a month to six weeks to save their company from Rader's clutches seeps through to Pigeon and his friends, and suddenly they are galvanized into action.

An emergency meeting of the board of directors is called. It is decided to seek another marriage partner or to buy a company that would conflict with the business of Rader's company so as to create a Justice Department violation. Investment bankers are called in and given forced marching orders. Meanwhile, the phones begin to beat a steady cacophony of offers to help, offers to merge, offers to sell out to them, offers to buy parts of them, offers to find offers.

Despite the feverish activity, nothing seems to fall into place. Target Company's higher than normal stock price discourages some suitors, and Rader's tough reputation as a fighter discourages others. Days go by; weeks go by. All the while the hectic trading in their stock continues. The morale of Target's employees disintegrates. Work efficiency plummets. But the arbitragers (the chicken hawks of Wall Street) are having a field day. The go-go funds are jumping in and out of the stock. Some of the company's oldest stockholders are selling out. Others are indicating that they will go for the Rader exchange offer. Some of the bank trust departments that hold their stock are beginning to worry about their fiduciary responsibilities.

Then Rader's S-1 prospectus is approved by the SEC. He gets a court order forcing Target to give him its stockholder list. Half-page newspaper ads in the key financial areas make public the exchange offer, and letters from Rader go out directly to the stockholders. In two weeks the game is over. The minnow has succeeded in swallowing the whale.

Did it have to happen? The answer is no. Target helped it to happen. Management, in the classic manner of the ostrich, chose to put its head in the sand rather than face up to a course of action alien to anything it had ever studied at business school. And many of the unquestioned old myths of business collapsed for Target executives under pressure of the new reality.

Among the tried and true business principles they had faithfully followed was the steady broadening of their stockholder family. It had taken more than forty years to reach the stage where they were able to exult in the wide sweep of their company's ownership. Target's list of over 25,000 stockholders now extended to every state in the Union and several nations abroad. A corollary business maxim that had warmed the cockles of Target management was the fact that not more than 2 percent of the company's stock was in the hands of any one holder. Here surely was people's capitalism incarnate, the very thing those Stock Exchange officials had been exalting for years.

And then there was that sly sense of security they had begun to feel several years before when their treasurer first pointed out how understated the company's assets were and how cleverly hundreds of thousands of dollars in taxes on the true value of the company's real-estate holdings were being avoided each year. They were comforted in the belief that if things got a little rough in the profits column some year they could sell off some of that real estate and flesh out the emaciated earnings column.

Even their smooth management hierarchical system was a model of corporate correctness. Only last month Mr. Pigeon gave a speech at the chamber of commerce luncheon during which he proudly told the audience how every first-line management executive at Target Company had come up from the ranks and averaged more than twenty-five years with the firm. Most of them had never even worked for another company since college. Loyalty and tight team spirit—the solid American virtues— are what the company had been built on.

But the good old days are gone. In this fast swinging new era of financial community relations, all those old verities collapsed in the face of the ultimate test: corporate survival. Present patterns indicate:

—Very broad stockholder ownership of a company makes it easy for a potential raider to pick up stock quietly while he is forming a base for the attack.

—The absence of any large holdings of a company's stock, particularly among top officers and directors, means there is no strong ownership group to oppose the raider when he surfaces with his attack plan.

—Understated assets may fool the tax collector, but they do not fool some of the shrewd Wall Street analysts who may be helping the raider pick his next pigeon.

—Inbred corporate managers may tighten the noose around the company's neck, for in their innocence they will find it very difficult to believe that anyone would want to rape them so boldly. Even when the signs become alarmingly obvious, they will insist—like lemmings—on going on with business as usual.

In this particular case, given the fact that Target management's stewardship did not rate the highest marks for deploying the company's assets at their optimum, or for moving the company into some of the more promising growth areas of American business, management should have been conducting a systematic program for developing potential marriage partners to shore up their weaker areas. Even if Target did not find instant love in that quest, it might at least have located an acceptable mate in the event that someday they would be in the market for a shotgun wedding.

Furthermore, Target's forward planning or corporate development department should have been continually evaluating smaller companies for potential acquisition. These acquisitions, made for stock, not only serve to dilute the position of any potential raider, but also tend to place blocks of company stock in friendly hands.

If Target did not have much authorized but unissued stock, it should have gone to its stockholders at the next annual meeting to request authorization for a substantial increase in the number of shares that could be issued. This can be a valuable and flexible tool once it is suspected there are outside designs on the company. Remember, a company can acquire other companies for up to 20 percent of its outstanding stock without stockholder approval or registration with the SEC or the New York Stock Exchange (although actually the Exchange gets interested when the number goes past 18 percent on any one deal). Three or four such acquisitions and the raider's position is diluted almost by half.

During all this time, Frank Pigeon's team should have been getting closer to Target's stockholders to gain their confidence and loyalty. Aunt Minnie in Dubuque and Uncle Joe in Rapid Falls, multiplied many times, have much to say about the outcome of a takeover bid. Management should have built an effective two-way financial communications team and kept the channels to their stockholders and the security analysts open. Surprise is a key element in an outside takeover attempt, but only a delinquent manager allows his company to be ambushed.

The point is, there are some basic precautionary measures that can be taken once a possible raid is suspected. Examine the corporate by-laws. If there is a provision for the calling of special stockholder meetings by a segment of the stockholders, consider eliminating it. Few state corporate laws require it, yet many companies gratuitously provide for such a meeting in their by-laws. This could well be misguided corporate democracy in today's fast-buck morality, for it plays into the hands of the outside raider. If the raider has to go to the banks to acquire a major portion of his victim's stock, he is going to want to effect his takeover as quickly as possible so that he can get his hands on its assets and use them to pay off his debts. If he knows he may have to sit with his high interest, borrowed money stock for many months until the next stockholders' meeting, he may think twice about the advisability of the attack.

Also, because speed of reaction is important, always have at least one emergency set of stockholder envelopes available—fully addressed, updated, and ready to be stuffed with a letter (but kept under lock and key). When a raider breaks his news in the press, he will get the headlines; the victim's answer will come at the bottom of the article. It is imperative that embattled management get its story directly to the stockholders as soon as possible after the raider's public announcement and that it tell its story completely and effectively. Management has the advantage of not having to clear that first letter with the SEC, so it should make the most of it.

Compile a list of the company's largest stockholders, those holding 1,000 or more shares. Contact these people directly by phone, asking them not to tender their stock until they have analyzed the whole situation. Management may even be able to indicate orally that a better merger or affiliation with another company might be on the way. Keep on close terms with the company's stock specialist. If there is unusual action in the stock, he should be the first to spot it. Whatever suspicions he has, it is important to know about them. As in any war, forewarned is forearmed.

That it *is* a war is not an exaggeration. Plunged into a situation where they must fight to preserve their company's independence, the company officers soon see many of the elements of war unfold before them. Spying and betrayal of their plans to the attacker may reach as high as the board of directors. Duplicity and weakness of character may be revealed by top corporate officers under pressure of the potential loss of jobs.

One thing is certain: if a company becomes the object of some acquisitor's raid, the lives of its top people will never again be the same. Whether or not they succeed in beating off the attack, the compromises, adjustments, and changes they will be forced to make will ineluctably alter the course of the company—and usually not for the better. Some companies that have succeeded in beating off repeated attacks by raiders have found their life's blood sapped by the continuous need for defensive maneuvering.

It used to be said that the corporate raider performs a valuable function in our economy by keeping company managements on their toes and forcing them to do a better job of running their businesses. That is as much nonsense as saying that the Red Chinese create a healthy atmosphere in the Orient by forcing the United States to take an interest in the smaller Asian nations. The raider is an aggrandizer, often ruthlessly motivated by an advanced state of egomania. He generally adds nothing to our economy, but a great deal to his personal exchequer. Extraordinary steps may have to be taken to protect the company, the management, and the stockholders from the raider's clutches. For the company's custodians to do less than their utmost is to pave the way for their corporate extinction.

3 / Advice from an Aging Conglomerator to His Nephew upon Graduating from the Harvard Business School

A secret microphone, hidden behind a potted plant in the library of the Union League Club in New York City, recorded the following mono-dialogue, which you will recognize as the sort of thing that is never reduced to print.

MY BOY, I PROMISED MY SISTER—YOUR MOTHER—THAT AT the proper time I would help set you on the road to prosperity. I believe that moment has come.

You have graduated now from the Harvard Business School with a distinguished record after a fine undergraduate career at Amherst. You have decided to enter the business world to earn your fortune and make your mark. The question is what direction should you take to maximize your chances, to get what you want in the shortest possible time.

Life runs in patterns; so does the business world. In the early forties, engineers and production men rose to the tops of their companies more often than other types because there was a great premium on producing, producing, producing. After the war, when everybody seemed to know how to make everything and raw materials were no longer

22

in short supply, the emphasis shifted to selling. Soon, marketing men began to overshadow production men in the battle for corporate command.

By the late fifties, the marketeers had done their work so well that their companies had grown too large and complex for most salesmen to manage, and then the money men —accountants and lawyers—began taking over the top spots. It seemed that they were the only ones who could cope with the legal and financial intricacies involved in complex dealings with governments and other businesses.

Companies continued to grow, often by swallowing up competitors and controlling their sources of supply. Seeing the specter of monopoly, the federal government began to crack down more frequently on companies that strengthened themselves this way in the marketplace. Soon it became impossible for any company already of fairly substantial size to acquire or merge with other outfits in any of its normal lines of business. So in order to maintain their growth rates, companies began reaching outside their normal lines of business. This resulted in the emergence during the sixties of a new type of company known as a conglomerate, meaning a heterogeneous mixture of parts seemingly growing big just for sheer bigness' sake. And the man at the helm was a multi-industry merger master, or conglomerator.

I remember only a few years ago, my boy, one of my standard lines, when appearing before security analysts' society meetings, was to describe my company's diversification plans as extending only in those areas of business where our production, marketing, and distribution know-how and facilities could make positive contributions. "Natural diversification," I called it, and as an example of unnatural diversification at its worst, I alluded to Textron. If our stockholders wanted a mutual fund, I said, they could buy that directly. They did not need an industrial company acting as their agent.

But gradually I came to see the error of my ways. Because the government was making it impossible to grow in any other way (except by the slow internal process), the crazy Textron way became the *only* way. To run this new type of mishmash company you had to become a card-carrying schizophrenic. That, however, seemed the new high road to success. I was too old and set in my ways to undergo the basic training course needed to become a true conglomerator in the most modern sense. Oh, I made some moves in the right direction. I bought up a knitting company and a children's book publishing company to go along with our basic heavy machinery business, but my heart was not really in it. I knew I lacked the true zeal of the really successful conglomerators, who almost without exception are twenty to thirty years younger than I and bound by no tradition whatsoever.

Now I suspect you, my boy, are much more suited for the role. You have imagination, quick wit, and a gambling instinct. Furthermore, ever since I've known you you've been a cold fish. Self-centered and ruthless. Perfect type-casting for the latest version of conglomerator: the takeover artist. Don't be offended. I mean it in the most complimentary sense. Remember that unlike any top management executives of the past, the raiding conglomerator must never develop a sense of identification or satisfaction with the goods or services *produced by* the business. Only the balance sheet counts. Learning too much about the details of any of your businesses will just clutter up your mind with needless technical garbage. That, you see, is one of my fatal flaws. I care about the quality of the machines we make. And sometimes I even worry about the people who make them, for I have been to their homes and have seen how they live. That can be even more dangerous.

Take my advice. Stay as mean as you are. Don't undermine your objectivity. It can take your eye off the ball.

Now if I were starting out with your assets —youth, education, wit, and drive—I would take my first job with a management consulting firm. That is the quickest way to get an inside view of how business operates and all the mistakes that are made. Three or four years at the consulting game and you'll learn all the industrial jargon you'll need for the rest of your life. You will also be able to spot your first target.

That is very important. You must get a base from which to build. Perhaps with some of your mother's money and some more borrowed from banks you can start buying into a relatively small company that has one successful

product and seems to be growing rapidly. It would be helpful if the company is listed on one of the exchanges; but most likely it will be an over-the-counter outfit. If its name has an -onics or -ography ending, that, too, would be helpful. But if not, you can change it when you own it. Once in control of your little -ographic beauty you can start to operate. Apply for listing on the American Stock Exchange because their rules are easier, and hire a hotshot public relations firm to pump out a lot of stuff on your research developments. Be sure you have a research director with a lively imagination who has no trouble projecting your technology into 1980. Every time you think you have developed a new product, announce it promptly. It may have material economic consequences, and the SEC does not want corporate management clamming up on significant developments. The last thing you want to do is create shady insider situations!

All of this should start the ratio of your company's price as compared with your annual earnings on an upward escalator. This is the key set of numbers in the whole game. The higher your price-earnings ratio the bolder you will be able to act. This early period while you are developing your p-e is sometimes called seasoning. A couple of years or so of this seasoning and you are ready for your leap into the big time.

Study the field carefully and find an old company with conservative management, good dividend payout, low price-earnings ratio, heavy assets and resources, and one that is generally depressed as compared with the rest of its industry. The ideal target company will have recently had several quarters of declining earnings but is now beginning to come out of its slide. Don't forget to do your research carefully and compile a dossier of management failures for possible use in ads and letters to the company's stockholders.

Chances are good you will find your target among the property insurance companies or the metal miners. Perhaps a medium-size bank or finance company. In any case, be sure to find a pigeon where no individual or group controls more than 2 percent of the outstanding stock. And for usefulness later, its assets should be at least ten times greater than those of your own company.

Start buying slowly. Don't run after the stock. Try to pick it up at your price. Buy as little on up-ticks as possible and buy through Street names in several parts of the country. In that way, no one will suspect that a stock accumulation is taking place. Even the computer chart technicians won't spot it. All the while you are buying the pigeon's stock, its dividend will be paying most of your interest costs, so you will suffer no hardship.

When you have amassed just under 10 percent of the company's outstanding stock—and, by the way, be sure you do not go over the 10 percent mark or you will be subject to the insider's rule and all your subsequent profits could be confiscated—you can make your first move. If you are not feeling gregarious, don't even bother to meet with the chief executive. Just call him up, and tell him who you are and what you intend to do. Then give Dow Jones your news release announcing your intention to make an exchange offer for all the company's outstanding shares.

Oh, yes, I should have mentioned that before you execute this gambit you should retain a top law firm skilled in preparing stock registrations and in working with the SEC. For as soon as you announce your intention to tender, the law firm submits the S-1 form, or red herring (so called because the first page is printed in red), to the SEC. A speedy approval by the commission is very important, so your registration must be without flaws. The more time you take in registration, the more time your pigeon has to marshal its forces. While it is good form to announce your intentions to the target's management before making them public (so they cannot tell their stockholders that you never informed them), warning them well in advance of your action is likely just to cause resentment and could break down the fine surgical atmosphere in which you should operate. Personal feelings and animosity tend to vulgarize the whole affair. Very unprofessional.

But the most important reason for conducting as little negotiation as possible with your intended victim is your need to have the element of surprise working for you. As in any war, surprise can neutralize potentially superior forces. Your pigeon will flutter around ineffectually for days after you hit him with the surprise tender. If you can manage a cash tender, the ball game will be over before he even gets untracked. You could wrap it up in two or three weeks. But I assume your target company will be far too big for you to attempt a cash tender, especially if times are like the current when money is rather tight.

So you can use the paper method, which has come into far greater vogue now than cash tendering anyway because of its unique advantages. While it takes longer going through SEC registration, it can be made as a wholly or substantially tax-free exchange. Cash is always taxable, and, therefore, has a disadvantage. The paper you will offer may be subordinated debentures with a high interest rate. This is set to give a much greater return to the target company's stockholders than the dividend currently being paid. The face value of these IOU's is also set at 25-30 percent higher than the price your victim's stock is selling at. If you want to add still another sweetener, you can tack on a convertible feature to the debenture or throw in a fractional warrant. Remember, warrants cost you nothing, and convertible features only slightly dilute your stock. The high debenture interest rate is effectively cut in half because it is a deductible business expense, while the dividend that you collect on your pigeon's stock is 85 percent exempt from taxes due to the intercompany dividend regulation.

Despite the obvious allure of your generous offer, you are sure to encounter stubbornness on the part of the company's top management. Unless you have been lucky enough to find truly yellow-livered specimens, the management will recoil at first and plan to recommend that their stockholders reject your exchange offer as "not being in their best interests"—that favorite defensive lawyer's phrase. To forestall this opposition, you might offer each of their key people very handsome salary increases. First extend the velvet glove, but keep in readiness the mailed fist to show them that it is off with their heads if they should oppose you, and you win anyway.

Occasionally even this does not work with irrationally dedicated top management. So you must reach beneath them to a passed-over senior vice president for your corporate informer. Find a man in the organization who is not personally wealthy, who has worked hard all his life, has not had the advantages of a gentle education and who is probably unhappy with the way the company has been run lately. This kind of man does not want to risk losing everything he has gained on his way up. He is afraid that in case of a complete takeover by you he might lose his job. He reasons this is too great a risk. As he thinks about it he even gets a little *resentful* that company management is demanding blind unswerving loyalty to them in this moment of crisis. What have they done for him lately? he asks himself. This man could very well be amenable to keeping you filled in on management's plans for opposing the tender, in exchange for a promise of a secure spot at the top should you win. He would view this as shrewd hedging.

If the game gets really rough and you need to undermine the morale of your target's management, imply that you have an extensive fifth column within their organization, a coterie of people who are anxious to see you move in. A little judicious wiretapping—there are several agencies that can arrange this for you quite easily—will turn up inside information that you can let drop casually in a meeting with your opponents. This is guaranteed to shake them to the balls of their feet and may even convince them that the tide is running too strongly for them to continue to resist.

Another rocky area for you may be the flak sent up by Congressmen and perhaps even home state Senators who fear losing an important enterprise from their constituency. Anticipate this and have your legislative representatives explain that you have no intention of moving the company. Indeed, you hope to expand the company's operations in that state.

Once your exchange offer is approved by the SEC you must move promptly. If the management will not give you their stockholder list, take them to court. You will surely win and the judge will order the list turned over to you. But do not depend on the list alone. Put big display ads in all editions of the *Wall Street Journal,* the *New York Times,* and the leading papers in the city of the company's headquarters. Make your tender offer at least 25 percent in value above the current market price of the company's stock. And make the tender period no more than two weeks.

One little trick I have learned to insure victory: get the performance mutual funds—the go-go boys—buying the other company's stock by the yard so that they can turn it in to you for a quick profit. To insure their interest, manage somehow to let advance word of your intentions leak out to a few of them. This can be done on a golf course, at a cocktail party, or wherever you find it most convenient to pass on really important information. The fund boys appreciate that kind of information and they know what to do with it. The SEC and congressional committees are beginning to get wise to that sort of thing, but they have never been able to pin it down legally. But, speaking of the SEC, I should warn you that they are trying to get tougher in this area and several Congressmen are trying to help them. There may be some new laws and rules laid down in this area soon, so waste no time while the field is still ripe.

But what if, despite all the correct moves you make, management opposition is so irresponsible that they hysterically run to another company for a shelter and virtually give themselves away to avoid being taken over by you? That is one of the hazards of the game. However, you can usually salve your affronted sensibilities with the knowledge that you have driven up the pigeon's stock by 20 or 30 points and you stand to make a tidy bundle with the stock you have acquired both on the market and through your tender. It's sort of a "heads you win, tails you win" operation.

If, however, you should manage to take over this company with your little pipsqueak shell, then you are really launched among the big boys. You will have taken over a company with many times your company's assets. Some of those assets, whether in the form of reserves or stock portfolio, can be used almost immediately to start discreet buying of stock in your next target. This time you can go after really big game, perhaps a company in the half-billion to a billion-dollar class.

Remember, my boy, think big and act big. America is a land of opportunists—er—opportunity. Happy hunting.

4 / Kiss and Tell on
Romantic Wall Street

THE CUTEST GAME ON WALL STREET IS KISS AND TELL, AND any number can play . . . for any number of reasons.

It started catching on late in 1968 with the Texas Gulf Sulphur case, when the U.S. Circuit Court of Appeals reversed a lower court decision and ruled in favor of the Securities and Exchange Commission on most of its tough charges of insider violations, that is, special advantages taken by company executives with privileged information at the expense of ignorant stockholders and potential investors. That jolted the Street, and the SEC's follow-up punch to Merrill Lynch a few days later floored them all over Broad and Wall.

Suddenly "immediate disclosure" took on powerful new significance and "inside information" became a sinister expression. In corporate boardrooms across the nation hurried conferences were called to discuss the meaning and ramifications of the new muscles developed by the SEC. Corporate law counsel and public relations counsel were called in at hundreds of publicly held corporations to review all their financial information practices.

In many companies the immediate reaction of top management was to clam up. Their reasoning was the less you said, the less you exposed yourself to legal action. Still other companies decided never to talk to security analysts or large investors without a public relations representative or lawyer in the room. No predictions, no specific projections were allowed. If by accident any bits of material information happened to slip out to an outsider, a press release would be prepared instantly and given general distribution to let everyone know what was going on.

The key word in all this was "material" as it applied to information. What precisely was material information? Obviously, forthcoming quarterly earnings figures were material, as was a new ore strike, because when these facts became known the stock market was likely to react to them. And so possession of this sort of information in advance placed a person in a position to make a tidy profit in the market. But was a new product about to be launched material? Was a new research director about to be stolen from a competitor material? Was a conversation on a golf course with an official of another company about merger prospects material?

Reporters asked SEC officials for a definition of "material," but the replies were evasive. One SEC official scheduled an appearance before the Practicing Law Institute and the $100-a-plate dinner played to a standing room only audience. Hardly a man alive on the Street could remember when so many lawyers parted with so much money for one lousy meal. The subject of what to disclose was obviously hot. The best definition extractable from federal officialdom seemed to be that material information was any information about a company's status or operations that would or could convince a prudent investor to take some action with regard to the stock.

Now that takes in a lot of territory. And as it permeated the consciousness of corporate managements and their financial counsel it began to take on a variety of subtle implications.

The Commission and the Stock Exchange were trying to protect the little investor. Aunt Minnie in Dubuque and

Uncle Joe in Rapid Falls have no access to inside information. Therefore, the Commission reasoned, they could be caught buying something which in reality was no longer what they believed it to be. And similarly they could be inveigled into selling what they owned not knowing that their company had changed. Certain insiders would know, but they must not profit therefrom. Aunt Minnie and Uncle Joe had a right to know as soon as possible after the officers of the company themselves found out, and certainly as soon as the friendly downtown banker or trust manager.

Though in many quarters the immediate reaction had been to clam up on financial information to avoid legal involvements, some of the real deep thinkers began working it over and began to see how the new more stringent requirements for revelation could have salubrious consequences in certain cases.

For example, this scene not too long ago in a paneled ankle-deep carpeted boardroom on Park Avenue in New York City was an ironic direct consequence of the new rule of reveal.

PRESIDENT: Gentlemen, I called this meeting to tell you that I have received a telephone call from Mr. Ephraim Rader of Inter-American Industries, and he requested a meeting with me for Thursday morning. I, of course, had to agree. He said he had something of great importance to discuss with me.

FINANCIAL VP: Omigod. That bastard. He's just finished digesting Holly Tool. That means we're next.

CORPORATE SECRETARY: I knew somebody would come after us. I knew it. I knew it. I've been telling you we've got to get our price-earnings ratio up.

PRESIDENT: Quiet, Henry. We all know that. We've

known for months we're a sitting duck. We're earning less than our industry average. We're loaded with assets. And all the directors and officers combined don't own 1 percent of our company's stock.

EXECUTIVE VP: We've got to get some stock out into friendly hands.

FINANCIAL VP: Too late. Rader'll be here on Thursday. That's the day after tomorrow. Chances are he already owns 5 to 10 percent of our stock.

JUNIOR EXECUTIVE VP (the one who just recently got elected to the post): Why don't we bluff him off? Tell him on Thursday we are already near completion of a major merger.

PRESIDENT: He'll see through that trick.

JUNIOR EXECUTIVE VP: Not if you make a public announcement of it. As a matter of fact, I believe we are obligated to do so anyway under the immediate disclosure rules.

FINANCIAL VP: Chief, you remember that talk with Alexander of Northern Loading?

PRESIDENT: You mean last spring in the sauna bath in Locust Valley?

FINANCIAL VP: You told me Alexander said a combination of our companies might make a hell of an interesting deal.

PRESIDENT (warming to it now): And I saw him again over Labor Day at the Hamptons and he reminded me of it.

JUNIOR EXECUTIVE VP: I don't think we have the right to keep this from our stockholders.

CORPORATE SECRETARY: Merger discussions over a period of five months. This should be reported to the Stock Exchange right now.

FINANCIAL VP: The Stock Exchange can be told that

discussions leading to possible merger of the two companies are under way. Simultaneously we should phone Dow Jones and Reuters, then put out a press release.

PRESIDENT: I think I'd better tell Alexander.

FINANCIAL VP: What if he doesn't want to mention it yet?

JUNIOR EXECUTIVE VP: He has no right to keep it concealed any longer. We are required to reveal this.

PRESIDENT: He'll think I'm crazy. It was in a sauna bath . . .

JUNIOR EXECUTIVE VP: Think of the impact on Ephraim Rader. Northern Loading has two billion dollars in assets. Thirty percent of its stock held by the Alexander family. This hits the papers tomorrow, a day before he comes in to see you.

FINANCIAL VP: Think how much more pleasant Rader's likely to be.

And so it was done. The president called Alexander, told him he felt obligated to inform the Stock Exchange and the press before any further rumors about their discussions developed. He also told Alexander of the imminent visit of Ephraim Rader. Alexander said he understood and gave the president permission to issue the release. He himself would inform his own board. That's the least he could do, he said, for a fellow club member in distress.

The news of the merger talks between the two big companies hit the broad tape early that afternoon. Trading was halted briefly in both stocks, and then opened again a couple of points higher. Ephraim Rader, not prepared to take on an already alerted opponent with a strong-armed ally at his side, canceled his date with the president due to a suddenly necessary out-of-town trip.

Three weeks later, Rader announced a takeover attempt against another company. A week after that, it was announced by the president and Alexander of Northern Loading that merger discussions of their two companies had been terminated. When questioned by an enterprising reporter, the president sadly indicated that the two companies decided there could be no proper "fit." Within a few days the stocks of the two companies settled back to their premerger "talks" levels. And presumably everybody involved will live happily ever after. Except for a few investors who happened to have gotten caught in the violent churning action of the stocks of the two companies those last several weeks. But that is the price of frankness and openness.

Not only is kiss and tell the order of the day, its companion—tell it like you truly think it is—is also gaining new adherents.

Say you are a company official whose company has developed a new product in a new line of business. In the past you would have test-marketed it quietly, perfected your selling themes, and then launched it regionally or even nationally. If it caught on, you would have your promotion people trumpet it far and wide. As for discussing it with the financial community, that would wait until you saw the effect it was having on your sales and earnings picture.

But now you wonder if that is the proper sequence of events. After all, this unique new dietetic chocolate egg roll has a potential market of 100,000,000 dieters and 40,000,000 Chinese food addicts. It is a whole new genre of product for your company, which has hitherto specialized in dog food and birdseed and has had a flat earnings curve for years. A new subsidiary has been formed to market the new product, and there is talk in the company of moving into the dietetic Chinese fast food franchise market, which would tap into the hottest thing in the eating business today. Your financial people are privately predicting doubling and tripling of earnings.

Now you are faced with it. Does management have the right to play it close-mouthed while word of the potential of this sensational new diet food product may start to leak any minute? If it should hit the nation's grocery stores and cause a sensation, as some insiders are already convinced, could management be guilty of having withheld these sensational projections from the investor public in order to benefit just the inside few?

The safest thing to do, you decide, is to call a press conference with the financial media prominently represented, and issue a statement admitting to the vast sales and earnings potential of this revolutionary new product. Lay out all the economic and fiscal parameters and introduce the company scientist who developed the egg roll accidentally when straightening up the mess caused by his three-year-old daughter in his upstate hunting cabin.

This, after all, is full disclosure and it is in the best interests of all your company's stockholders. Especially if the company's stock takes off after the press conference.

And then there is the conglomerator who has been quietly picking up some 400,000 shares of Company X. This amounts to 5 percent of Company X's outstanding stock. He has done his homework well and he knows that Company X is loaded—it has a book value based on actual assets that is several points above the current market value of its outstanding stock. He has also been careful in his buying not to reach for the stock and possibly stimulate it, but to accumulate it gradually and let it rest in its normal sluggish price range. This type of buying may have taken him a little longer than usual, but the absence of effect on the price has justified his patience. One day in the course of a conversation with a *Wall Street Journal* reporter this careful conglomerator lets drop the fact that he owns a chunk of Company X and some months ago he met with management of Company X. But he will not admit he is now considering a tender offer for several million additional shares.

The WSJ reporter recognizes an Abreast of the Market piece when he sees one, however, and he enterprisingly writes it up when he gets back to his office. Next day, when the item appears, Company X's stock reacts wildly. From 42 it moves up to 46 on heavy volume. Then Company X's president issues a statement that no serious discussions have been held with this gregarious conglomerator, nor are there likely to be.

The WSJ, hot on the trail, gets back to Friendly Conglomerator, and asks him to comment on the Company X president's statement. He shrugs it off and allows as how he considers Company X an excellent investment because it is greatly undervalued. Up another three points goes the stock to 49.

Three days later, Friendly Conglomerator calls in the press and reports he has instructed his counsel to begin the necessary preliminaries prior to filing with the SEC an exchange offer of his company's debentures, new issue preferred stock and warrants valued at 68 for Company X stock. Up five more points goes Company X.

Now the frenzied activity begins in earnest. Company X management scurries around frantically searching for a marriage partner. In a few days one is found. The new swain is persuaded to make an even sweeter offer. He swings in with a statement that the enamorata is worth 72 of his convertible debentures and warrants. With a bidding contest shaping up, the arbitragers start to move in. Up goes the price of Company X stock to 58.

A few weeks go by and Friendly Conglomerator's

completed registration is cleared by the SEC and he makes his offer public in full page ads in the *New York Times* and the *Wall Street Journal*. The surprise is an increase in the paper he is offering for Company X stock. Several security analysts interviewed by the press estimate the value of the new offer to be in the neighborhood of 74 to 77. More feverish trading in Company X stock, which crosses 60 all the way to 64.

Undaunted, and stimulated by Company X breathing urgent sweet nothings into his ear, the favored fiancé gallantly bumps the pot to an 80 valued offer.

At this point, with the stock of Company X nearing 70, Friendly Conglomerator folds his cards and agrees to sell out his stock to the big stick at 78. He admits defeat, he says, for he knows when he is up against too much power. Since he originally bought his 400,000 shares at an average of 42, Friendly Conglomerator is forced to salve his wounded pride with a 36 point profit, or a total of approximately $14.4 million. And to think it all started with an open-handed expression of interest to a financial reporter.

For a while there seemed to be a startling increase in the number of these expensively administered defeats of potential raiders. Fortunately the disclosure regulations force it all out in the open for us all to see, while the "defeated" raider slinks quietly away, crying all the way to the bank.

5 / Semantics for the Swinging Executive

THESE ARE PARLOUS TIMES, BESET WITH CHANGE AND BE-devilment. Things are almost never what they seem, people hardly ever are who they say. Signposts of the past serve mainly to mislead, and labels tried and true are now frequently either out of style or out of sync.

Pity the hard-working businessman who has to spend an increasing portion of his life assessing and reassessing his environment just to make sure he is not becoming outmoded. How can he find the time to keep up with the fluid semantics of our day? And yet somehow he must, if he is to protect himself in this fast-changing world.

To help make his life a bit less difficult we have set down on the following few pages a kind of beginner's guide to the corporate word maze. This, then, is a businessman's Baedeker to today's swinging scene.

Corporate image and *corporate identity* are terms of deep concern to thinking businessmen across the country. With psychiatry for individuals somewhat on the wane, psychoanalyzing companies to determine the reflection they cast in economic life is becoming the vogue. You have a real treat in store for you if you have not yet had the corporate identity oratorio played for you by the real experts, complete with continental accent. Before the full-fledged identity performance is over you will have learned how unphallic is your *corporate symbol,* how sinister is your slogan, the true meanings conjured up by the words in your corporate name, and how pitiful are the colors in your trademark. You will wonder how your company ever made it so far selling products under that sick suggestive logo of yours. It may even be insinuated to you that your company has been embarked for some time on an unconscious course of corporate suicide.

Still, all hope is not lost, you will be informed by the corporate headshrinker. Somewhere within the scope of your company lies the answer. The right acronym, the proper rhythm in your corporate credo, the precisely true shade of blue behind a sturdily masculine new logotype may yet save your company from Gehenna. Just sign up now for this new corporate orgone box (with a bow to Wilhelm Reich), and with your fees you may be led out to new high ground.

One of the most commonly bruited-about characters recently is the *gunslinger*. Not from out of the Old West, but often from the Lower East Side comes this heroic figure. Of course, it is not his speed with a gun but his quick moves with a pencil in balance sheet territory that gains him his sobriquet. And his dexterity of finger is matched by the rapidity of his mouth. Whether it be in the managing of a fast-action mutual fund or a fast-grabbing conglomerate corporation, the gunslinger moves swiftly and tells about it just as fast. His legend grew rapidly in Wall Street while the market was rising. But of late some of the fastest gunslingers have been badly burned. For example, some of the *go-go guys,* who manage the so-called performance mutual funds, seem to have gone too far in their quest for fast action and have been shot down by owners redeeming their fund shares faster than the slingers can sell them. And some of the gunslingers managing the fast-grabbing conglomerates arc being left high and dry as their *poolings of interests* (the technique of figuring balance sheets of acquired companies as if they had been part of the acquiring company the whole year of the acquisition and thereby melding all the sales and profits together) are being drained away by their suddenly high-principled accountants.

Still, the gunslinger is a man to watch. Whether he hits or whether he misses, he keeps things stirred up around the Big Casino.

A businessman is not really with it these days if his language is not liberally sprinkled with computer argot and space-age vernacular. It is not even enough to be able to use

that old saw joke about the limitations of data processing: garbage in, garbage out. He should *get the signal* when conditions are right and be prepared to move when *all systems are go*. He is in danger of being considered gross if he does not know the value of an *interface* (bringing together of disparate talents) with his associates when vital decisions are at stake. Time and speed of communicating is a constantly preoccupying problem. The modern businessman develops a virtual fetish about it. He is always indicating concern to shorten the *turnaround time* it takes to get answers back on questions he poses. If he could learn to *multiplex* better, or get his message out on two or three channels simultaneously, he knows he would be more efficient. In the final analysis, though, it is the *real-time* problems—those that must be solved on the spot—that make him or break him.

Even as general management people have become infected by the computer syndrome, marketing people have become entranced by the professional football world of dynamic tension. A sales executive will proudly refer to his *hard-nosed* approach to a problem, meaning he thinks he is tough-minded and determined. An advertising type may offer to hit a competitor with a *blitz* or a *red-dog,* meaning an unexpectedly massive surprise attack in a vulnerable area. One wonders if the rather sedentary lives led by these highly competitive marketing men force them for their own self-respect to overstate the viciousness of their occupation.

Pro football terms even pervade their strategy conferences. In one boardroom on Madison Avenue recently, a sly character recommended test-marketing a false product in a remote area of the country to *fake-out* the company's competitor—that is, mislead him—while the company prepared to launch a national sales campaign, according to the *game plan* for the true new product. "While they're taking our fake, we'll *throw the bomb*. We'll get the *points on the board* before they learn which way to the end zone." Presumably, all those points mean dollars on the bottom line.

You are certainly not *relevant* today if you are not talking *ecology*. Every thinking person during some part of his day must be able to crease his brow and mutter toneless imprecations about the deteriorating state of the human environment.

The *quality of life* is what it is all about. That is the catch phrase that incorporates the total concern. You hear it wherever you go. Man has been living on the crust of the earth for thousands of years, but only in the last half decade or so has he come to realize that all that messing around he's been doing will eventually do him in. And not eventually, either. Soon. Maybe in twenty or thirty years if all goes along at the present rate.

Somehow business has become the prime culprit in this centuries-old rape of the world. But the guilt feelings for it all seem to have become more highly developed in the United States than in almost any other country. Hence, the wiser American businessmen are realizing they had better start making the proper sympathetic sounds if they want to avoid boycotts, sit-ins, sabotage, discriminatory legislation, and social ostracism. Yet at the same time they do not want to cut their profits by spending much to change their production facilities or radically altering their products. So they do a lot of *objective research*. Thus, for example, the fuel companies accurately point out the inefficiencies and dangers to the atmosphere of the automobile internal combustion engines, and the auto companies complain of the impurities inherent in the fuels supplied to motorists. Each industry thoughtfully engages scientists and engineers to help improve the other's product for the good of society.

Meanwhile, the more euphemistically sensitive companies launch not pollution control but *environmental quality* programs. They refer to the *emissions* from their plants rather than pollutants. And at least they do their best to reduce the size of the particles so they are harder to see, as well as cutting the odors in order to offend fewer passers-by. Still, the basic problem of emissions goes unresolved as thousands of factories of all kinds continue to belch out their unburned wastes. And so even as the sounds of consternation rise, our air gets thicker.

What's happening to our rivers and lakes is a subject of as much concern to the public as our air. Waste flooding out of grimy factories into pristine mountain streams is a favorite antibusiness cartoon subject even in the local weekly shopping gazettes. The thinking businessman today who finds it difficult to change the basic operation of his plants hits on some compromise measures. He landscapes his factories, tints the *effluence* a refreshingly blending turquoise, and sends his plant managers on community speaking tours to point up the costly changes he is making as his part in improving the town's quality of life.

When these good Samaritans talk to concerned community leaders they affirm the importance of *water resources management* as described in all their company manuals. They avoid if possible any discussion of the hot liquid their factories have been pouring out, which has changed the whole balance of piscatorial life in the local streams. But if pressed they admit they are studying this *thermal enrichment* and say they will have an answer soon.

Yet environment is not all air and water. It is also sight and sound. The soft drink and beer makers who used to be delighted to count their empty bottles and cans along the highway as just so much more good brand advertising now recoil in horror at the sight. Such is the rapid change in public attitude that they now realize every wayward empty is a threat to their very existence. And so they turn to the can makers and bottle makers and demand that they devise containers that self-destruct rather than survive and deface the countryside. Meanwhile, the packagers and the pack-agees all get together and support programs to fight litter and keep our deteriorating land as beautiful as ever. But how to attack the underlying problem—the slothfulness of the basic American slob—is too dangerous for any industry to consider publicly.

As for high sound levels, otherwise enunciated by the pundits of ecological doom as noise pollution, that topic is just now coming into its own as a subject for dire public concern. The degenerating effects of our pounding high-decibel civilization on our genes and our brains are beginning to be hinted at in gravest terms. War, disease, and disaster are only some of the conditions now considered traceable to excessive noise in our environment. Because noise control is rather pedestrian, some of the more elegant companies have taken to referring to their abatement pro-grams as *sound attenuation*.

Before this newly surging public concern has run its course many of the so-called advances of civilization in such diverse fields as travel, entertainment, and nutrition may be turned around and set back generations in time. Such is the public mood, however, that thoughtful business-men feel if they do not talk and act properly regressive they may be in great danger of being left vulnerably in the van-guard.

You know the old-fashioned word, *cyclical*. You know that when analysts use it to describe your business it does your price-earnings ratio no good. It conjures up a picture of an earnings curve that looks like a picket fence in a slum area. Well, you have recently hired a young financial adviser who has friends among the new Wall Street whizbangs. He says you ought to think about moving your company out of its humdrum industrial category where the price-earnings ratios usually move between 9 and 12. He says you have to get your company considered a *special situation*.

But how to achieve this vital reclassification? Simple, says your adviser. Pick up a little -onics company, and maybe announce a research development that will use industrial sludge in a highly sophisticated engineering control system. Automatically, he tells you, you're out of the dull tool class and into the high technology area, where thirty and forty times earnings abound. He has some friends who virtually guarantee a couple of quick brokerage house market letters, and he even thinks he can do something through someone he knows at Standard & Poor's.

All very enticing. But before you make the -onics overture or rev up your research director, consider what may happen after the opening publicity blast. Your acquisition may earn less per share than your own company, thus diluting your equity, and its scientific strength may run head on into comparable know-how by bigger companies. Your sludge control system is admittedly three years away from practical usage, by which time controls may be out altogether with hermetics the hot item. The better analysts, the ones who take a little time to work out the probabilities, may actually come up with the thought that you have weakened your basic business by spreading your scientific and management talent too thin. Result: bottom of the list of formerly reliable tool companies.

Does the sight of a well-proportioned symmetrical table-of-organization chart give you a little thrill? Does it give you a feeling of orderliness, rectitude, precision, muted violins playing, a fire crackling in the hearth? Well, you are in deep trouble, baby. Deep personal trouble.

This is the day of *free-form management*. Organization charts that look like Christmas trees are very out. They are signs of the dead past. What's in and living is *synergism* —getting the most juice out of the interaction of your parts. And you cannot maximize your return on assets and optimize your intramodule synergism by old-fashioned one-over-one-over-one organization lines. You've got to keep the channels fluid. Indeed, if you really want to swing out there with the leaders you should forget about organization charts and hire some hyphenated professor at Harvard, MIT, or Stanford to start building you a *corporate model*. This is the current *sine qua non* with the most advanced management scientists. All the most respectable *multi-industry pluralistic* companies have them. Sometimes a whole department of people guard them and tend to them.

What you do is order one built for your company for, let us say, fifteen years hence. Your own corporate model is the structured vision of your company fifteen years from now in the world as it will exist then. Along with your particular blueprint comes a mathematically reasoned roadmap of the terrain you will have to traverse between now and then. All that is left for you to do is to assemble the prepared parts and fit them in like a jigsaw puzzle along the way.

There is a great advantage in having your own tailored corporate model. It gives you a sense of direction, a feeling of grand purpose. And if some obstreperous stockholder should question you on a hard-to-explain acquisition or new product introduction you can always interpret it in terms of your grand design. You can tell him it was all carefully worked out and programmed to fit in with the corporate model you are working toward. Who would question it further? Long-range planning runs neck-and-neck with motherhood and God in the business world nowadays.

Just as long-range planning, corporate models, free-form management, synergism, and *congenerics* (a more euphemistic form of conglomerates) are in these days, *tippers* and *tippees* are very definitely out.

A tipper is an insider in possession of important information about his company who gives out that information to a friend. The friend, who recognizes the value of this information and buys or sells stock in the tipper's company, accordingly is known as the tippee. These two characters are involved with something called 10 b-5, which sounds like a running play called by a pro football quarterback but is actually an SEC rule. It is the rule that imposes restrictions on inside information if that information is *material*. Just exactly what is material has never been precisely defined, but it is generally understood to mean that sort of information which, if revealed, would likely have an effect on the market price of the company's stock.

The new strict enforcement of this rule, as signaled by the Texas Gulf Sulphur, Merrill Lynch, and Glen Alden cases, makes the tipper guilty and punishable even if he himself does not profit from the use of his inside information, and the tippee guilty and punishable for taking action in the stock even if the information did not particularly influence his decision.

Investment bankers who sit on the boards of directors of corporations are placed in a rather peculiar position. They are naturally privy to inside information in that company. What are they to do if clients ask their opinion of the company? Obviously, they must take the Fifth Amendment. By all logic of 10 b-5 as now interpreted, they or their firms should never become involved in any stock offerings of corporations on whose boards they sit. Because of this, a number of investment bankers have recently resigned their directorships. They see it as the only way to clearly avoid the label of tipper and keep their market letters from being regarded as tout-sheets. This also allows them to continue to pick up the companies' investment banking business, but with a clearer conscience.

Do you remember the old guffaw that said an investor is a speculator who guessed wrong? Well, the era of the cavalier approach to your investors or stockholders is over. Its demise was hastened by the advent of the corporate raider. Relations with stockholders have taken on a great deal more importance lately. This, in turn, has encouraged the development of a variety of consultants who call themselves *stockholder relations specialists.* Some are good. But some are charlatans. You may be a setup for one of the latter.

Are you concerned about possible adverse stockholder reactions at your next annual meeting? Have you been plagued by some of the obstreperous professional stockholders in the past and this year you know your company has given them more ammunition than ever? Then beware the expert with the self-admitted commonfolks touch. Human Ed knows those gadflies personally, he will tell you. He can see to it that they ease up on you this year. As for the rest of the cattle—er—shareowners, he has the well-tested format. It always works. Cut out the box lunch and schedule the meeting for 9:00 A.M. And instead of a question-and-answer period show them a preview of a new TV show you're going to sponsor. Triple the number of guards, some in uniform and some in mufti, to hustle any troublemaker quickly out of the meeting room. And plant two little old ladies and a college professor type in the audience to get up at intervals and compliment far-sighted management for doing a splendid job under most trying economic and competitive conditions.

Seems to make sense to you, you say, and maybe you buy it. Pity. In real life it probably plays out like this:

Any hint in advance of management concern will turn out the entire first team of professional needlers. The earlier hour and no promise of lunch eliminates most of the nice lady stockholders who fear rush-hour traffic or have to get their children to school in the morning, so you are left with the hard, rotten core, who are never dissuaded. The questions from the floor start coming even before the corporate secretary calls the meeting to order. The TV film is hooted down with indecent remarks, and the first time one of your guards tries to muscle Mrs. B. out of the hall a near-riot ensues. To top it off, your little old lady stockholder plants forget their lines and the professor type is recognized as a refugee from an off-Broadway musical. The denouement finds you thanking your stars you escaped with your life, but the *Wall Street Journal*'s covering story the next day makes you wish you hadn't.

Moral—as that well-known philosopher, Fred Astaire, once said: "Smile, face the music, and dance."

And finally there is the great search going on throughout industry today: the quest for *creativity*.

In advertising who will come up with the next step after the homely models who belch into the TV screen and the psychedelic banana splits? In finance who will top the invention of the convertible subordinated high interest debentures (or IOU's) in exchange for old-fashioned equity securities or the use of lots of warrants (options to buy stock) in exchange for real common stock in the company to be acquired? The warrants are especially creative for they give something free to everybody: the stockholder gets a call option on the acquiring company's stock that could enable him to reap riches for many years into the future if the common stock grows; the corporation itself gets an inflow of funds when the warrants are exercised by the stockholder but meanwhile it does not have to show dilution of equity; and the institutions get to play with a big piece of low cost leverage in the Great Market Game. And in industry, who will come forward with the frontier-expanding concept to follow the sensational fast food franchisers who created instant millionaires after one-week chicken-dipping courses?

A company is just not hip if it is not doing something very special to release the creative juices in its executives. Merely sending them to special classes at the American Management Association or the Harvard Business School is old-fashioned. It must organize its own special programs. For example, one big Midwestern industrial company recently sequestered some forty of their top people as an *encounter* group in a plush resort lodge and put them through a variety of soul-searching exercises for a four-day period. One particular event required them all to close their eyes and crawl around on the floor of a big meeting room. They were told, "When you run into somebody else, touch and stroke each other and try to experience what the other person is like." The object there was to treat the group to a truly puerile experience in the hope of recapturing for them some of the uninhibited climate of creativity only children are capable of achieving.

Though that technique may not be quite your bag, you will have to find some way to pump an increasing number of new ideas into your company's bloodstream.

They say the game keeps changing, changing ever faster. And the rules keep shifting, and it is harder to tell the players without a scorecard. If it all seems just so hopelessly upstream to you, however, think of the guy farther back. He does not even have a paddle.

6 / To Rock a Mockingbird

THIS IS A HORROR STORY—A MODERN AMERICAN BUSINESS gothic. It all started with a letter addressed to the chairman of the board.

> *Dear Mr. Wolfe:*
>
> I have followed your career in newspapers and magazines for years. I know you are a fine man and your company is one of the leaders in its field.
>
> But for the past several months my company has been quietly accumulating your company's stock. I see it happening because I work in our accounting department. We already have thousands and thousands of shares of your stock.
>
> It's unfair. Our people intend to keep buying as long as they can buy your stock in its current low range between 20 and 25. As soon as the supply there dries up they intend to make a tender offer for the rest around 30. They plan to take you over.
>
> I don't think this sort of thing should happen any more in this country. The people in our company are mean, vain, and avaricious. I know what has happened to the people of other companies we have taken over. I don't know what you can do to save yourself, but I couldn't live with myself if I didn't at least warn you.
>
> I wish you all the luck you will need.
>
> [Signed] *Sympathetic*

It was early on a Monday morning. Hiram Wolfe had opened the letter himself because his secretary had not yet arrived at work.

He read the letter a second time. Then he examined the postmark. Mailed in New York City. That told him nothing. Wolfe read the letter a third time. It had obviously

been typed on a home portable typewriter, not an office machine.

A crank letter, he told himself. But yet . . . what if it
were true? That damn Chickasau Knee Joint Division
foul-up was bringing company earnings down to the lowest
point in five years. The stock of his Amalgamated Datonics
had dropped over 65 percent in less than eight months.
Faster than almost all the other conglomerates, which as a
group had dropped more than most of the market. To make
matters worse, some of those damn analysts were beginning
to needle him about his overly optimistic forecasts and with-
holding of vital information.

The s.o.b.'s are turning on me, he thought. First they
practically beg me to give them big figures so they can get
their fund friends interested, then when they see I've missed
the mark by a few cents they start calling me a fake and a
liar. Maybe some bloody analyst is helping mastermind a
takeover of me. That would be some bloody joke. Raiding a
raider! It's never happened before . . . but there's always
a first time. The more Wolfe thought about it, the more he
realized how vulnerable he had become.

Even at the current 23 I am selling at more than sixteen
times last year's earnings, Wolfe thought. When the Street
hears earnings are dropping from $1.42 to $1.10 I could
fall below 18. Maybe even worse if they begin to suspect our earnings picture for the future. A cold sweat began
to break out on Wolfe's forehead. His left eyelid began to
twitch as it always did when he got nervous, and he felt a
sudden need to go to the bathroom.

By the time he returned he was convinced that someone or some group was truly out to get him. Maybe even
some lousy Establishment banks are in on it, he thought.
They're always mouthing off about how takeovers are bad
for our economy, but they've been bending their principles

awfully easily lately to make a buck. And now all of them are reorganizing into one-bank holding companies. They're all getting set to get into the takeover game themselves.

Wolfe considered his spot. Amalgamated Datonics had twenty-four diverse divisions ranging from junk metal pro-

cessing and computer leasing to soft drink bottling and ladies' undergarment manufacturing. These divisions were all hung onto the original company in Hackensack, which made private label radios and television set parts for Japanese manufacturers. Wolfe had gotten control of the radio company seven years ago, changed its name from Jersey Broadcast Equipment, Inc., to Amalgamated Datonics Corp., and gone big-game hunting.

In a half-dozen years he had gobbled up eighteen major companies, having engaged along the way in three cash tender raids and four "Chinese currency" takeovers, where he offered handy combinations of his inflated common stock plus convertible debenture and convertible preferred. Five of his marriages were of a shotgun variety where the bride succumbed because she had already lost her honor, while six of his alliances had been fairly amicable. That is, they were amicable until he got control and fired almost all the top management. For the record, however, he had brought the company from $14 million a year sales to over $700 million, from a total market value of $8 million to a current market value of over $580 million (based on his Amalgamated's 25.2 million shares outstanding and last closing price of 23⅛). And only last year his stock had been as high as 68. Still, his holding of 900,000 shares was worth over $20 million in today's market. Pretty nifty for a thirty-nine-year-old orphan from the wrong side of the Chester, Pa., tracks.

But in the process of putting together what *Business Week* once termed one of the three fastest growing conglomerates in America, Wolfe cut something less than a Byronic figure. Building by bloodletting was what the *New York Times* termed his technique once he took over companies. He unleashed the little wolves in his kennel and they ripped the organizations apart, selling off assets, suing suppliers and slow-paying customers, and decimating the entrenched old-line management personnel. One Wolfed company saw 107 of a 112-man corporate staff axed within a month. As one furloughed executive remarked, "I was prepared for rape, but this is genocide."

Yet as long as Amalgamated's earnings per share kept growing healthier, Wolfe could scorn the unfriendly remarks and refer one and all to the ultimate scorecard—his balance sheet. He allowed no one in his company but himself to talk to security analysts. At that game of riposte and parry he considered himself a virtuoso. Wolfe recognized the value of favorable financial page publicity, and he was forever urging his public relations consultants to "get more bullish stories." He liked to be interviewed, and in truth the press considered him a good subject because he was usually quick with a colorful or acerbic remark. And his track record was a spectacular one. Until recently.

It was early last year when the big trouble started. As you might expect, trouble in Wolfe's lexicon meant bad price action. The basic problem actually surfaced several months prior to that when his vaunted automated knee-and-elbow joint construction plant in Chickasau, Texas, began spewing out faulty parts. Wolfe fired the plant manager and his entire staff immediately, but an emergency engineering team from New York headquarters could not solve the problem. Meanwhile, dealers and construction companies were screaming for rebates. The loss ran to millions of dollars.

Wolfe transferred money out of reserves to cover up the loss and the analysts did not at first get suspicious. Then a construction trade publication ran a story on the "automated disaster" growing in the Texas Panhandle. That led to some analyst questions which taxed Wolfe's virtuosity. He began to find it difficult to control his temper, and discordant sounds regularly crept into analyst interviews that had previously been dulcifluously orchestrated. Some bearish reports on Amalgamated Datonics began to appear among the financial services, and the Street's *enfant terrible* soon became its terrible bore as Wolfe accused his critics of malicious character assassination and irresponsible analysis.

That was when he also started ducking interviews and calls from the press. He was often "out of town" or "unavailable for comment" as relayed through his public relations people. They told him he was wrong, that he should at least call back. But Wolfe thought he knew better. Then a couple of financial magazines did unfavorable articles on the prospects of Amalgamated Datonics, the breakdown of its internal quality and cost controls, the severe morale problem that had developed among its middle management personnel, and the mounting plant community problems it was having due to its caustic methods of personnel reduction.

As usual, Wolfe reacted swiftly. He fired all his public relations people.

But Amalgamated stock continued to slide. It went from its high of 68 eight months before to 22, its lowest mark in more than five years. Last Friday the stock closed at 23⅛, having touched the low point again during the day. All week long there had been unusually high volume, but up till now he had only considered it from the aspect— albeit unpleasant—of selling pressure.

If someone's out to get me he will never have a better chance than right now, Wolfe thought. My stock is way down and I have a very bad earnings report coming out in the next few days. Convinced now that something foul was afoot, Wolfe began to move with characteristic speed. First, he decided he would tell no one of the anonymous letter he had received. No good getting anyone else in the company nervous, he thought. Also, he was not absolutely certain which of his top people he could trust.

Wolfe buzzed his secretary, who by now had arrived and was making his morning coffee, and told her he would take no outside calls that morning. Then he told her to have the treasurer come in immediately and alert the corporate secretary that he wanted him to stand by for an urgent meeting in a few minutes. Wolfe had decided on an aggressive defense using every trick ever used effectively against him in the past, along with a few even he had never come up against.

Step one was to get his stock moving up so that the raiders would have a harder time picking it up. Albert Riddle, the company treasurer, who was also trustee of the employee pension fund, was told to start buying Amalgamated stock for the fund that very day.

"You've got almost $5 million to use," Wolfe said. "Our stock is very low. It's a good buy now for the employees. Buy at least 20,000 shares every day this week. Buy 5,000 just after the opening and 15 to 20,000 between two-thirty and three o'clock."

"That could look like we are painting the tape," Riddle said.

"Then make it look like something else!" Wolfe shouted. "I want to move our stock up. And don't give me any morals or ethics arguments either. This is employee money and what's good for the company is good for their jobs. I say our stock has to start moving back up for all our good. You see to it that most of your buying is on up-ticks. And if the market softens, go in and buy some more. But don't use company money. We may do that later. Use several brokers; use Street names. I don't care how you do it. But I want to see an unbroken string of plusses at the closings all this week."

Then the corporate secretary–general counsel was given his orders.

"Van Lingle," Wolfe said, as he puffed on a cigar and stood gazing pensively out his thirty-third-floor Park Avenue window, "I have decided that in these tempestuous times, with everybody and his Dutch uncle taking potshots at conglomerates from Wall Street to Washington, it is the better part of valor to put our ship in the soundest possible shape."

Whirling from the window and scowling at the bespectacled Van Lingle, Wolfe said, "There're some new things that have to go into our proxy. First of all, we are moving up the date of our annual meeting. Our annual report and proxy will be mailed in ten days and our annual meeting should be held the minimum fifteen days thereafter."

"Why so fast?"

Hiram Wolfe decided he at least would have to tell his corporate secretary of his fear of a possible raid. "I have a hunch," he said, "that some envious scoundrel may see in this moment of adversity for our company an opportunity to move in on us. I want to get the annual meeting over with before he is able to get a tender offer in and out of registration."

"That's good thinking."

"Wait'll you hear what else we're gonna do," Wolfe said. "We already have our by-laws fixed so that only the board of directors can call a special meeting of stockholders. Well, I now want to go to a staggered election of directors. Only one-third of the directors elected every year. And on top of that, we will switch to cumulative voting. So even if an outsider grabs a big chunk of our stock he'll only be able to elect a fraction of a third of our board because, if worse comes to worst, we'll concentrate on two out of five up for election. That would still leave us ahead twelve to three.

"And then," Wolfe continued, his voice rising in pitch with his growing excitement, "and then we'll put in a proposal to amend our certificate of incorporation to require an 80 percent vote to authorize merger or consolidation with any company that owns 10 percent of our outstanding shares."

"The Exchange doesn't like that sort of thing," Van Lingle said.

"If I weren't a gentleman I would say something unprintable to that," Wolfe said.

"Anyway, it's a two-edged sword," Van Lingle said. "It could hinder us in future amicable negotiations."

"I'll worry about that then. So is a staggered board more of a problem in flexibility. But I have more immediate concerns. You get on now with a new draft of the proxy with all these things in it. It has to be completed and ready to go in a week, because of the pushed-up date of the annual meeting. So hop to it."

As soon as Van Lingle left, Wolfe began another phase of his defense plan, one that he was to continue for the next several days. He picked up the telephone and started calling friends of his who were fund managers or customer's men with large discretionary accounts. He told them to begin buying Amalgamated because something big was in the works. He put his personal reputation with them on the line in a way he had never done before. And he asked for the kind of favor you can ask for only once. But he felt he never before had needed help so much. So, he was going all out—cashing in all the gratitude credits he had accumulated over the years. Still, he had to protect these people somewhat. He could not bring out really bad annual figures now. He decided to use his ace in the hole and trans fer into earnings the proceeds from the sale of three buildings he had made during the year. He had previously planned to move those several millions into reserves against certain possible real-estate losses rather than incur the heavy income taxes, but he needed them now to keep from reporting a sharp earnings decline. Wolfe called Riddle again and instructed him to so inform the accounting department.

In the days that followed, the forced buying in Amalgamated Datonics moved the stock up against a generally soft market. The loaded proxy statement to shareholders went out with all the new proposals. And the rushed-through annual report went out showing a modest earnings *rise*—with the help of a big, nonrecurring item.

During a rare moment of permitted relaxation just one month to the day since he first initiated his aggressive defense, Wolfe, surrounded by several of his top staff, felt the need to do a bit of crowing about the swift, incisive actions he had taken. "You gotta get up awful early in the morning to beat old Hiram Wolfe to the worm," he said.

"You can say that again, chief," Riddle said.

"We're the talk of the Corporate Secretaries Society," Van Lingle said. "I was at one of their meetings yesterday."

"What were they saying?" Wolfe asked.

"Oh, how they couldn't understand why you'd want to tie yourself up so much so suddenly."

"They didn't figure, of course, that it might be some other sucker we tied up in knots, did they?" Wolfe chuckled.

"That's why they're the secretaries and you're the chief," Riddle said.

All present laughed at the sage remark.

"Say, something kind of interesting came up at the meeting," Van Lingle said. "Several of the men reported their chief executives got a real weird letter about a month or so ago. Some guy claiming to be tipping them off that an accumulation in their stock was going on prior to a surprise tender offer. It was a well-written letter, not like the usual nutty types. One of the men's president had a few very anxious moments until he checked around and discovered several of his friends had also gotten one."

7 / Pigeons in Peril

LONG BEFORE GEORGE ORWELL WROTE HIS FABLE OF THE *Animal Farm* twenty-five years ago, Wall Street had become accustomed to dealing with its own particular menagerie. There were the raging bulls and the bleak bears, the haughty lions and the meek sheep. And always there were lambs in abundance ready to be led to slaughter. Sharks have traditionally loitered around the edges of the Street eager to be of service to all manner of beast.

Lately there has arrived on the scene a new denizen of the glass-and-concrete forest. Actually, this bird has always been around, but it is only recently that it has gained prominence. It comes in a variety of shapes and sizes, from small and well-proportioned to very large and grotesque. The over-all genus is termed: pigeon.

The pigeon is not to be confused with the sitting duck, a creature so masochistic it virtually asks to be devoured. The sitting duck is usually accommodated by small-time or garden variety vultures. No, the pigeon is not always that obvious. It is probably an outfit that may well have been leading a fairly normal life in the forest of the Street. It may even have done a little devouring of smaller pigeons in its time.

Today's pigeon is a rapidly multiplying breed because the nature of the world it lives in has changed so rapidly. Nowadays it costs so much more than ever before to build a new plant or establish a product brand that seizing them in full flight has become simply the economical thing to do. As for pigeons with more eggs in their nest than they know what to do with, well, there are plenty of furry and feathery fellows around to help lighten the load for the "good of society."

So the predators and potential predators, fed by success, have escalated in number. At the same time their newer, more sophisticated ways of identifying their prey have forced the Street to make a sweeping reclassification of its wildlife.

For the relatively uninitiated in the way of the wild, this is a partial compendium of some of the more common types of pigeon that are in dire peril in the light of today's business conditions—conditions that saw some 4,400 merger actions in 1968, far more than in any previous year, with the rate in 1969, despite the slowdown caused by the tight money conditions, up another 37 percent and 1970, which started off more slowly, picking up rapidly in momentum as money eased toward the end of the year so that 1971 has started off on a rising crescendo of merger activity once again. A great proportion of these mergers have been loveless amalgamations to help victims escape the clutches of attackers. While some pigeons may well be preserved from a takeover fate by new restrictive legislation and tougher enforcement of current regulations by the Justice Department and the Federal Trade Commission, the overwhelming majority remain in greater peril than ever before.

Let us look first at one particularly fat and turgid specimen. Basic International Foodstuffs is a grocery manufacturing company with many brands in national distribution. Its annual sales are approaching a billion dollars, but for the last several years it has been growing at a rate lower than that of its industry and its return on equity has actually been dropping faster. Slipping, too, has been the share of market that many of its brands command. It has not introduced an important new product in five or six years, yet it has been spending between $8 and $12 million in research and development in each of the last several years.

During that time it either missed entirely, or got aboard very late, virtually every major trend in food consumption. Most of its products adapt poorly to the calorie and cholesterol consciousnes of the American public. It has hardly an entry in the fast-growing snack foods category. And while several of its branded products fit admirably into the center of a meal, it has no connection with the fastest growing of all food areas—the quick food service franchised chains.

Not a single officer of this sixty-six-year-old company has been with the organization less than twenty-five years. Few have worked at any other company. Some years ago, a fairly venturesome chief executive tried moving the company into some new product areas in conjunction with some foreign food companies. He was so carried away by those potentialities that he became quite loquacious and expansive at security analyst society meetings and in private conferences with money managers. Many articles on this former chief executive appeared in the financial magazines and newspaper business pages. His public relations people were very active. He received so much personal publicity and spoke from so many prestigious platforms that he became an acknowledged leader of his industry.

The company, which once had been dubbed "the bank that manufactured food products," began to be looked upon as a special situation in the normally slow growth, defensive grocery products category. Its price-earnings ratio rose to the top level of companies in its industry.

But not for long. The gourmet lines of European and Asian food specialties looked very good on the supermarket shelves, but they looked good for too long. Their major movement was from eye-level shelves to foot-level shelves, then off the shelves altogether. It seems most people's tastes were not yet sufficiently developed to appreciate the kind of puréed eel, essence of frog's legs Provençale, and marinated squid the company was pushing.

And, sadly, the new multiflavored, noncarbonated soft drinks were being forced upstream just as the torrent of carbonated dietetic soft drinks was cresting in from the South. Result: a big fizzle-out at the cash register.

And so it went. The elegant promises of the ebullient chief went flatter than yesterday's pancake mix. Down,

down plunged the p-e ratio; out, out went the ebullient chief. In came new management up from the ranks but in the traditional mold that this company had known for years. That is, do not take risks, accumulate cash against a rainy day, rely on the good old standard products, and— above all—never paint a rosy picture for the stockholders. Look what happened with ebullient Dan, the high-roller man.

So here the company is today. Plants throughout the United States and thirty-two nations abroad. Several well established and profitable, though not leading, household branded products. An institutional and industrial food business growing at 2 percent per year but capable of a much better rate. A glass packaging subsidiary with good facilities and costs commensurate with its industry. Almost no debt, assets of $600 million, and thousands of acres of land, carried on its books at virtually nothing. Add to that $70 million in cash and marketable securities. Its 32,000 stockholders are in every state in the union and some twenty-five nations abroad. Fourteen million shares out-standing and no director or officer owns more than 30,000 shares. The total stock owned by all officers and directors is less than 3 percent.

Watch out fatso, there's a guy out there with fricassee in his eye and he is measuring you for his pot.

A pigeon of quite a different feather is this building materials company. American Forest Products' main items are tract contractors' staples—various composition boards and inexpensive floor tiles. As in the case of our previous specimen, this company has relatively little debt, thereby in-suring sizable borrowing power for any successful raider— borrowing power with which the raider can pay off the debts he incurs in the course of acquiring the stock necessary to take over the company.

This target bird has unique appeal for an aggrandizer in its vast potential in the building materials business, which seems slated for excellent growth with the almost certain housing boom of the next decade. It is one of the leaders in its product lines, has modern plants, and is generally as well situated as any company in its industry. Its earnings growth has been good but not spectacular.

But it has a terrible secret. For many years it has been known as a one-man company. The chief executive was an innovator, an organizer, and a driving marketing force. Security analysts were impressed with him, fund managers swore by him, the financial press treated him with respect. Five months ago, Mr. Number One suffered a stroke. The news was kept from the papers and he was moved quietly to a private rehabilitation center in a little New England village. While he convalesced, a team of three executive vice presidents—a production man, a marketing man, and a financial man—ran the company. They tried to do things the way the chief would have done them, but they disagreed among themselves. Each, of course, hated the other two even more than he ever had hated the chief, and each schemed now to position himself so that he could be the clear-cut successor if the chief should not make it back.

Meanwhile, the reports from New England on the chief's condition were discouraging to his wife and children, but encouraging to the unholy triumvirate. The chief had trouble remembering anything farther back in the past than his breakfast. He found it difficult to button buttons or to get both his lips synchronizing on words of more than two syllables. And his vaunted golf swing had gone completely to hell. Truly, he was in bad shape. Few in the company beyond the very top level of management knew of the serious condition of their chief. Those who did had been sworn to absolute secrecy because of their fear of what would happen to the stock if the market learned of the peerless leader's condition.

As the days of his absence from the executive suite grew to weeks and the weeks lengthened to months, the stories invented to explain away his nonappearance grew increasingly more elaborate. And the infighting among the three would-be crown princes grew ever more intense. Middle management men who had a good view of the action and some flexibility within the company began to speculate on who would be the eventual winner and began to line themselves up with their choice. Thus, the company began to split into three contending factions, each trying in subtle ways to stymie the plans of the other two.

Mix now into this cauldron of turbulent corporate comedy, the one ingredient sure to turn it into a tragedy: the informer. He is high enough up in management to see what is going on, not high enough to affect the result to suit himself, but sly enough to see a cute way to pick up most of the marbles for himself. The more he thinks about it the more he likes the sound of it: president of the subsidiary. First a phone call, then an early breakfast meeting at The Plaza with the famous Ephraim Rader, then . . . another bird joins the taxidermists' hall of fame.

Inside information is often the undoing of many unsuspecting pigeons. It strips them of their protective drab exterior and reveals them to the corporate voluptuary in their true sensual nature.

For example, there is the humdrum industrial chemicals company whose sales have never reached the $100 million mark in its more than forty years of existence. General Chemical Additives, Inc., makes and sells a variety of bulk resins, acids, foams, acetones, and other commercial elixirs. Hardly a heady combination.

One point of attraction, though, is its enviable liquidity position. Its current asset-to-liabilities ratio is almost 3 to 1. Furthermore, its stock is actually selling at well below book value. In order to save money on research and development, it has practiced for years a policy of endowing several university laboratories with grants for special experimentation. In that way it has kept its scientific staff and plant overhead down while keeping itself *au courant* with technological developments on various campuses across the country.

Who would have guessed that one of their score or more grants-in-progress would come up with such an exciting development as the almost certain cure for chicken pox? Indeed with a touch of poetry, for it occurred in a biology laboratory of the small Southern university alma mater of the company president.

Rejoicing was muffled as the company mustered its limited shekels to prepare for a crash program of development of a commercial product. It believed it had an ineluctable lead on all possible rivals with the rights to this marvelous discovery securely tied up for many years, but it did not want to stir up unnecessarily any substantial competition in the race to bring out the world's first chicken pox vaccine.

Pity that all this is about to be relayed to someone with quite a different clinical interest in a potential health drug bonanza.

A rather similar drama is ready to unfold around Deep Hole Metals Company, a general minerals mining outfit. In this case the bearer of the crucial information is a disgruntled labor leader who has never forgiven Deep Hole for its ancient heritage of heavy-fisted guards and boiling water down the mine shafts. Small matter that the company has been run in recent years by a bunch of drones whose labor policy would have made Franklin Roosevelt sound like a Tory and who can barely stand the violence of the Green Bay Packers.

Seemingly Deep Hole is neither a leader in its field nor has it prospects for ever being one. It would offer no special takeover problem because its stock has gone nowhere for years, its price-earnings ratio is among the lowest in its industry, there are no big block holders to contend with, and of late its earnings have been sliding downward. As could be expected, the poison pen letters from stockholders have been steadily increasing in number and intensity. No, the takeover problem would not be great, but who would want it?

Enter now the self-appointed savior of the masses with a special tale to tell. And this tale is wrapped in dollar signs. For he has learned from a company geologist who absorbs too many martinis that Deep Hole is secretly locking up the rights all around the land outside a big Mexican city where it has made a discovery of possibly the world's richest supply of magnesium. A major ore strike in an area easily accessible to labor and transportation. Too much responsibility to be entrusted to this simple pigeon. Only a card-carrying vulture can handle this one.

The beasts downtown, you see, are all so considerate.

8 / Do I Hear a Motion to Adjourn?

IF WINTER COMES, CAN SPRING BE FAR BEHIND? WINTER means annual report time at publicly owned corporations across the country, and spring means annual stockholder meetings. Annual Headache Time, as it is more familiarly known in the offices of the corporate secretaries, whose prime responsibility it is to shepherd the company through this required obstacle course.

Once a year the managements of stock-owned companies must pay the piper for the many tax and sales benefits accorded them under United States corporation law. They must come face to face with the unwashed and the ignorant, made churlish by foul atmosphere and stung into hostility by professional rabble-rousers.

Even in good years most managements feel that the main purpose of the annual meeting is to adjourn. But in a bad year the usual ennui is replaced by plain old-fashioned fear. That is because the preparation of the annual reports proves to be painful experiences at hundreds of companies. And the annual reports set the stage and the mood for the stockholder meetings. In a year that saw precipitous drops in sales and earnings at many corporations whose managements never knew or had long forgotten how to report anything but record sales and compounding profits, the pain was pitiful. Now the declines, and in some cases actual losses, would have to be explained. The growth plans that failed, the new products that bombed, the automated tubes that didn't extrude, and the wells that came up dry would have to be accounted for. Because it was stockholder money that financed them. The stock prices that followed the earnings down have already alerted Aunt Minnie in Dubuque and Uncle Joe in Rapid Falls that all is not well in their corner of our great people's capitalism. The lugubrious annual reports soon to arrive in their mails would further inflame them.

While the public relations staffs work long, arduous hours to put the best possible face on some of the worst possible facts, the corporate secretaries and their staffs and outside consultants carefully prepare to cope with the day of reckoning. Some of the more thoughtful companies actually marshal and deploy their forces the way a professional football team develops a game plan for a crucial contest.

Step one for our typical Embattled Company is, of course, intelligence gathering. Scouts are sent out to attend other company annual meetings to see what are the most frequently asked questions this year and what are some of the new tactics being employed by the perennial gadflies to attract attention, cause havoc, and gain personal publicity. Full written reports are made, supplemented by tapes of the more lurid sequences. If a particular ploy or turn of phrase by a management executive proved especially effective against a noisy stockholder, that segment is rerun several times to absorb all the nuances. The Society of Corporate Secretaries also does a summary report of the most frequently asked questions at annual meetings, and the reports for the last ten years are pored over to get an accurate line on the styles of the chief tormentors.

Then films and reports of past Embattled Company stockholder meetings are studied and critiqued from the standpoint of what worked and what did not and how it could have been handled better. Some of these prep sessions get quite volatile, and injuries incurred, both physical and psychical, have been known to put men out of action for the main event.

Even as one team of staffers has been doing that research, another team, always including at least one dour representative of the treasurer's office, has been putting together a realistic list of the company's most vulnerable points during the past year. These are the areas they decide most likely to be attacked on Meeting Day:

—Profits were down, dividends were cut, but top officers' salaries rose on average 10 percent during the year.
Four top-level executives who were hired last year with three-to-five-year contracts at high salary levels have already been proven incompetent but cannot be removed because of clauses in their contracts.
—Several parking lot fires in the northeast were traced during

the year to the company's infrared car windshield de-icer.
—Generous contributions were made to charities where company officials served on the boards.
—Staggered election of directors continues with three directors now past seventy-seven, one of whom is palsied, another halt, and the third stone deaf.
—The new automatic ice-cube ejector introduced during the year with great fanfare had to be suddenly withdrawn from the market when several models proved so spirited in spewing out cubes that a squall of concussions and severe facial abrasions broke out around the country.
—Another year has gone by with no Negroes in management and the two showcase Negro secretaries in the home office recently quit out of boredom and embarrassment.
—Two sons of the president and a first cousin of the chairman of the board have moved up to division manager levels during the year.
—The five company planes were used on the average only 18 percent of the time for direct business trips, and the company's Maine hunting lodge was the scene of a terrible row when the executive vice president's wife caught him in a conference there with the advertising manager's traffic control girl, although only a small item on the mysterious destruction of the wing of the lodge later appeared in a local weekly.

It was agreed that this was only a normal list of imperfections but that certain sadistic stockholders would undoubtedly seize on many of them as excuses to hector management.

Now for the meeting plan to foil the ingrates. The intelligence squad and the analysis group get together and match up their conclusions. Recommendation number one, on which virtually all members of the commando team concur, is to move the annual meeting to the least accessible place possible. The few dissenters (mostly from the PR staff) point out that in recent years Embattled Company, along with many other large, publicly held corporations, has evolved a philosophy that views the annual meeting as an additional opportunity to tell the positive corporate story not only to stockholders but to the investment community at large. Consequently, the annual meeting had been moved to New York City and held the last several years in a large hotel ballroom in order to attract and accommodate larger audiences. Following the meeting, a full postmeeting report was customarily prepared and distributed to all stockholders and thousands of security analysts.

"It's corporate democracy in action," said one of the PR men, "and we should not suddenly reverse ourselves just because we had one bad year."

"Corporate democracy, my foot," said the assistant treasurer. "It's more like corporate suicide to go out there and let those slobs throw darts at us with the *Wall Street Journal* and the *New York Times* reporters writing it all down. And maybe even *Time* and *Newsweek* and *Business Week*."

The specter of a riotous annual meeting engraved in stone by the business press for the whole world to see won the day for the champions of retreat.

Return the meeting to the Corporation Trust office in Wilmington, Delaware, was the thought that came first to mind. After all, the company used to hold its meetings there until several years ago because it was incorporated in Delaware. Wilmington is a charming garden spot of the near South, and you can hardly get there from anywhere. For example, only two trains arrive from New York in the morning—neither before 10:15 A.M. Thus, a meeting set for 9:00 A.M. would force stockholders coming from New York City to get to Wilmington the previous night and stay in a hotel. To get there by plane from more distant cities one would virtually have to bail out while passing over the place.

Expensive and very time-consuming. Sure to eliminate many borderline-interest stockholders, but also to infuriate the more tough-minded who will manage to get there anyway and make life for company management even more painful in payment. Thus, a better idea is needed.

"Why not go the full route if we're going to move the meeting out of town?" says the new assistant secretary, anxious to make his mark as a corporate strategist. "The company was actually founded sixty-three years ago in West Kutztown, Kentucky, before it moved to Louisville. It's about time we showed proper respect for our origins and commemorated by holding our annual meeting there."

"That was such a tough town that even their canaries sung bass. Is it still on the map?"

"Who knows? If it's not, all the more reason to give it another chance. After all, it mothered this great company."

"There used to be only two freight trains a week stopping there on the way through the Appalachian Mountains."

"At least the place isn't *totally* inaccessible."

"Just one problem, though," said the second assistant general counsel sadly. "I believe there is a subpoena outstanding in Kentucky against our chairman for nonpayment of alimony. He hasn't been able to go into the state for over fifteen years."

And so a perfectly viable scheme is shot down in cold blood, and the corporate planners abandon the relocation gambit and turn to the basics of preparing their team for the frontal stockholder assault at the meeting.

It is decided by the group to stage a mock stockholder meeting with half of them impersonating irate and defiant stockholders utilizing all the known tricks of the professionals, while the other half plays the part of the top company officers trying to parry them by using the best of the standard diversionary and obfuscating techniques of corporate management and perhaps working out a few new tricks just for this occasion. The objective is to anticipate the worst that can happen and have the precise countermeasures prepared so that a total scenario can be presented to the chairman for his dress rehearsal with his directors and officers two days before the annual meeting.

For stage setting, one of the assistant secretaries reports to the group that he has arranged to have portable microphones carried by airline-stewardess-type girls all over the floor so that the professional agitators will not have to scream their questions up to the dais. However, a central control panel will be placed behind the dais, manned by a highly trained technician. If any speaker from the floor gets too long-winded or insulting, at a signal from the chairman that mike can be cut off. Furthermore, a technique learned from the chairman of IBM will be employed this year: raising the sound level of the chairman's mike in the event of an argument so that he can speak over any voice in the room without interruption.

A team of male and female sergeants-at-arms are to be stationed as inconspicuously as possible around the room. Only at last resort are they to move against a stockholder, but if it should be necessary and they get their signal from the secretary, they are well drilled in their assignments. Female guards handle female stockholders and male guards handle male disturbers. Firmness is desirable but physical violence is absolutely taboo. Meanwhile, two motion picture cameramen will be stationed in the balcony to record the entire scene for evidence to be used in the inevitable court case against charges of corporate brutality.

Then the questions start. Or rather, first the diatribe, for it is common practice for two or three of the professional stockholders who attend thirty to a hundred or so of these meetings to grab a microphone and launch into a series of derogatory remarks and castigations. Currently, according to the dope sheets, the professional agitators are *for* cumulative voting (votes per share equal to the number of directors being voted on, with the right of the stockholder to assign those votes in any proportion to one or several of the candidates) and preemptive rights (accordance of preference to a stockholder versus nonholders to subscribe to any new issue of shares so as to maintain his original proportion of the company's shares) and *against* staggered elections of directors, long-term contracts for officers, high salaries, generous bonuses and stock options, and corporate contributions to charities.

Whether or not the professional stockholders have proposals on the proxy form they will surely filibuster their favorite points. Most chairmen know the standard turnaways: staggered election of directors is more like the Senate method while annual elections are more like the House of Representatives, but in order to gain optimum usefulness from a director he should be assured at least a three-year term to learn the operations of the company; high salaries, bonuses, and stock options are necessary to compete for the best management talent to help run your company; a company has a social responsibility just as an individual citizen does, and if big companies did not support the most worthy charities the nation would be the poorer (wave the flag on the side of the angels, how can you lose?)

But the jackals will soon start to bore in on the specifics of this company. One corporate devil's advocate, impersonating a well-known lady stockholder, asks, "With earnings sharply down and the dividend reduced and the price of the stock way down, how come the chairman's salary went from $140,000 to $155,000 last year and the president's from $120,000 to $135,000? Why must only the stockholders suffer while you fat cats slop it up?"

Possible answer: "Madam, I am sure your husband's salary went up last year whether or not his company earned more. Economic conditions much beyond the control of any one company can have serious effects on earnings, but it wouldn't be fair to penalize individual workers for that. Bonuses, on the other hand, *are* geared to specific sales and earnings, and you'll note that bonuses in our company are in keeping with the lower tone of the year, even, I dare say, as in your husband's firm."

Possible retort from floor: "I'm not married, you big phony." (Which will draw a nervous laugh from the audience.)

Possible counter: "I'm sorry about that." (Which should get a bigger laugh and win over many of the neutral stockholders who will admire the chairman's urbanity and cool humor.)

And then the stream of questions about the imperfect products that got out during the year. One of the more histrionic stockholders might even come dressed in bandages to dramatize what happened to her (for some reason it is usually a her rather than a him) when she used the new automatic ice-cube ejector.

Possible reply from the chairman: "Only a small minority of the machines proved faulty, and they have all been corrected by now. We see a great future for this product. It is another in the continuous flow of new ideas coming out of our very creative research and development department, which I believe to be one of the tops in our industry." (One or two company shills in the audience will start a round of applause for this.)

A delegation of black militants might show up for the

specific purpose of challenging management on its discriminatory hiring practices as revealed by the low percentage of blacks in white-collar and management-level jobs.

Possible answer: "We have never counted up our employees in terms of color. We always seek the best man for the job regardless of color or religious belief. We are an equal opportunity employment company in statement, in belief, and in practice."

It is after a sonorous answer like that that the chairman might hear from some obscure but irate stockholder from the rear: "Do you realize what an ignorant vulgarian you are?" The consensus of this board of strategy is that the best way to handle that is calmly to ask for the next question.

Held in reserve for the truly difficult question is the nonanswer answer. The play starts with a triple lateral in the backfield to confuse and divide the charging stockholder, and ends with a reverse.

Suppose the question is: Why did the consumer products division lose more money than every other comparable company in its industry? First, the chairman smiles appreciatively and says he would like to call on the vice president of manufacturing. He then gives a little talk on how the company's production facilities are now the envy of the industry and then he passes the ball to the research vice president who talks about some of the company's new advances in compact living that may well revolutionize our whole quality of life. Then he hands off to the sales vice president who talks about the calculated risk the company has taken to leapfrog its competition in the battle for tomorrow's men's minds. "We are convinced," he says finally in measured tones as he completes the reverse, "that in 1969 we have laid the groundwork for an unprecedented surge forward in the decade of the seventies."

That type of fancy ball-handling will work most of the time. A truly obnoxious stockholder, however, might conceivably persist in trying to hold management's feet to the fire. A head-on power play from the chair may be the only solution. "Sir, you have come here to disrupt our meeting. But your past record of sympathy to Communist causes is well known to all these people as is your rather unique jail record. You are entirely out of order." Then cut the floor mike.

If the meeting starts to run too long with the fusillade of hostile questions showing no sign of abating, a recommended move is an announcement by the secretary that the luncheon is ready in the adjoining room and serving will start as soon as the meeting is over and that gift packages will be distributed to all stockholders on their way out after lunch. This is sure to stimulate the impatience of the vast majority of the stockholders in the room, especially the middle-aged ladies in the flowered hats who haven't been able to follow the trend of most of the questions anyway. They will start mumbling and perhaps even baiting the obstreperous few, who intend doggedly to persist in their questioning of management and hurling out quotable preprepared phrases for the press. The growing hostility to them by the rest of the stockholders often serves at least to divert their line of fire. The professional nasties often have to start defending themselves against the crowd. This is usually the beginning of the end.

In that type of spot, one of the well-known female management hecklers, microphone in hand, once turned to a nice little old lady who had mumbled something of impatience and said, "Shut up, you old hag. You're just jealous because I'm more beautiful than you." She was then roundly booed.

By this point it should not be too difficult for the

chairman to end the question period and call for the final count of balloting on the proxies. But in the unlikely event that the aisle antagonists are still undaunted, an ace in the hole might have to be trotted out. This would be the equivalent of the bomb in a football game.

It is set up this way. The secretary receives a whispered message on the dais from a well-dressed man who has rushed up from the floor. He then writes out a message to the chairman, who dramatically interrupts something he is saying to read it to the group. "Ladies and gentlemen," he reads solemnly, "I have just been informed that there is a person in the audience with a severely contagious case of spinal meningitis." (Pause to let it sink in.) "Do I hear a motion to adjourn?"

Amid the rush for the exits no one will even notice the secretary legalizing the meeting by quickly calling for the final count on the proxies before the session officially ends.

9 / Dear Andy . . .
(Department of Advice
to the Forlorn)

THE UTTER LONELINESS OF THE MANAGEMENT MAN HAS become one of the standard clichés of our time. Legend has it that this poor soul has no one to turn to with his most pressing problems. His closest associates cannot help past a certain point, for often they themselves are a part of his problem. And besides, he must always maintain with them a certain aura of urbane capability, sometimes called command presence or charisma. Even his wife cannot be a wholly trusted confidante for often she, too, is subtly competing with him for dominance right in his own family. So he must be careful not to reveal to her certain chinks in his armor.

If only there were some all-knowing, sympathetic personage to whom he could turn without reservation, even some businessman's equivalent of the familiar lonely-hearts columnist. What a boon to sorely beset management executives that would be!

Assuming there were such an Advice to the Forlorn columnist, here is a likely sampling from his early mail, along with the words of wisdom in reply to each missive.

Dear Andy:
I am fifty-one years old, have two daughters in good Eastern colleges and a charming wife, to whom I am never unfaithful. For fifteen years I have been in charge of market

research at my company, which I shall identify only as a large national manufacturer of consumer and industrial products. The function of competitive product analysis is also included in my department.

For the last three years our deodorant foot powder line, which is our leading consumer product seller, has been slipping in share-of-market. We were once number one, but lately we have seen two other brands pass ours and one very new one come up to virtually even with ours. None of us can find any quality of those other products that makes them superior to ours. Furthermore, they employ some of the most sickening graphics in their commercials I have ever seen, with background sounds by some of the worst of the modern pop music combinations.

But that is not what I am writing to you about. It is the accumulation of annoying slipshod incidents in my firm in recent weeks, which has begun to cause me considerable concern. I think there is a breaking down of our structure and team spirit, and I myself am beginning to feel it rather keenly. I have noticed, for example, that there is considerable carelessness in the manner in which memoranda are now routed to all of us vice presidents. I happen to have seen several general memos on some of my associates' desks recently that have had my name omitted.

And the cost-watching is beginning to go to unpleasant extremes. It takes days and several telephone calls to the supply room to get even a package of pencils brought to my office. Lunches in the executive dining room are being sharply curtailed, for I have not been invited to one in two months, whereas I used to get called at least twice a week. Even travel arrangements are affected. Without even checking with me our travel coordinator now invariably books me tourist class. Not being as slim as I was in college, sitting in a middle seat on a plane all the way to Los Angeles makes me feel like Quasimodo when I get there.

To show you how poor our internal communications have become, last week at a rather critical moment I found myself locked out of the executive john. It was all I could do to contain myself until I discovered that the lock had been changed the previous weekend when I was out of town, and the office manager had forgotten to give me a new key. It is that sort of slovenly management that makes me view with alarm the direction of our company.

And yet there are startling inconsistencies. Recently I have found personal things in my desk rearranged in orderly piles, someone evidently really caring about appearance. But what I consider to be a downright outrage occurred when my secretary was fired by the personnel manager for eating her lunch at her desk. Now really, that is an extremely gauche reaction, even if the odor of garlic in her salami sandwiches was getting a little strong.

Still, all of this could be overlooked if it were not for the

disgraceful mismanagement of this past Monday. I knew intuitively that I was in for a bad day when my train was delayed and I phoned the office to say I would be late. Of course, there was nobody tending my telephone since my secretary had been let go, so I left the message with the operator. She said, "Oh, Mr. C., I didn't know you were still here."

I assured her I most certainly was, but when I arrived at the office I discovered my desk was gone. I thought I must be losing my mind, but then I discovered it out in the hall. I immediately called Maintenance and reported what a gaffe the cleaning people had pulled and told them to move my desk back, but they said they could not without a requisition from the executive vice president. Though furious, I immediately sought to complete that ridiculous formality before the whole situation got utterly ludicrous. To my great consternation, our estimable executive vice president was tied up in a conference all day Monday. So I was forced to sit out in the corridor the remainder of the day. The next day, before I could get to him, he left the city for a series of meetings, according to his extremely frigid secretary. I asked her to issue the desk-moving requisition in his name, but she refused. So I continued to sit in the hall for yet another day, while the coffee wagon wheeled by and the office boys paused to rest their heavy stacks of mail on my desk. The following day there was still no change of venue, and my visitors had to sit out in the corridor with me.

Is this not a portrait of a company in severe decline? What can I do to arrest this alarming slide? I should be grateful for your candid comment.

Yours hopefully,
Chagrined

Dear Chagrined:

Surely you must be in the league with Wellington's cavalry officer, about whom it was said he was so dumb that even the other cavalry officers were beginning to notice.

Wake up, stupid. That's bye-bye they're waving at you in their not-so-subtle way. Chances are you're getting the treatment because you'll cost the company a lot more if they have to fire you than if you voluntarily quit. But why accede to their wishes? After fifteen years on the job you deserve to be treated like a higher-class animal. So while you're getting your résumés out, give them a few awkward moments with some homespun games of your own.

For instance, bring in your own coffee pot and undersell the Schrafft wagon. You've got a better location now than the wagon, anyway.

If they change the lock on the john again, call the Fire Department and tell them someone may be locked inside. The department has experts in opening doors without keys, though the doors themselves seldom survive the effort.

As for that sweet executive secretary and her satanic boss, the executive vice president—you can add immeasurably to their future relationship by sending her a warmly informative anonymous note telling her his wife has once again hired a private detective to record all her husband's extracurricular activities. Even if their relationship is pure as the driven snow, the "once again" line will at least get her thinking some graceless thoughts about him.

Dear Andy:

I just cannot stall another day. We've got to make a decision about our company name. The management consulting firm completed its depth analysis several weeks ago and made its recommendation. My public relations director has submitted his report based on two years of careful study, and my advertising manager has thrown on the table the consensus thinking of our four ad agencies. All their ideas seem good, but there is no unanimity. The only thing they all agree on is that our current name describes some other company. Rockingham Shoe Company doesn't fit us any more because we closed down our last manufacturing line in Rockingham four years ago and we stopped making shoes altogether two years ago.

Our management consultants say we're in the systems business and we should put that in our company name because it is a hot concept in Wall Street these days and it will pay off in the price-earnings multiple. But the only good system I really know about in our company is our accounting system, which keeps showing our earnings moving up while more and more of our product lines are becoming obsolete.

My public relations director says we're in the business of improving human life and it would be good for our corporate image if we were widely known for that. It would even help in recruiting at the colleges, he says, because it would make us seem relevant to the students. Well, if sneakers, contraceptives, pole-vault bars, and parking meter machines don't improve human life, I don't know what we're making them for. So I guess we've got as much right to that relevant label as anybody.

The ad agencies and my ad director, though, say our new name must have lots of *sell*, lots of drive, not be static. Movement, they say, is the key. Whatever we call ourselves, it should have motion, go. That's what moves products. Everything we do should be measured against how well it will move our products.

My wife has some ideas on the subject, too. She says we should coin an entirely new name, make up a word to sound like the twenty-first century when there'll be housing developments on the moon and outposts in northern Venus.

I just don't know. I just don't know. Everything they're saying seems to make sense. But on the other hand it does seem a shame to discard the old familiar name by which we're known on the Stock Exchange and which our founder gave us fifty-five years ago. After all, with everything spinning so fast in this crazy world, it is sometimes a welcome relief to find something solid and familiar and unchanging. Isn't there something to be said for good, old-fashioned stability? What do you think?

Sincerely,
Confused

Dear Sincerely Confused:

I marvel at your ability to hang on as long as you have. With Coolidge gone, Billy Sunday, and the rest of your friends no longer around, it must be quite lonely for you.

But you know there is a certain charm in our society, too,

once you get the hang of it. Though status quo-ing it may no longer be hot stuff, there's a new game these days that is really the cat's meow . . . and after the music goes round and round it all comes out the same.

It is called "relating." You have to relate what you're pushing to what society is supposed to need. Now, society is never going to get what it *really* needs, but it keeps looking for that something else it thinks it must have. That is what you must provide. Combine that thought with Contemporary Rule No. 4—you are not what you are, but what you seem to them to be. It is the map they admire, not the terrain; the odor, not the taste.

Thus, your company name should really reflect all the things you *should* be selling. If you aren't there yet, chances are neither is anybody else. Therefore, be the first on your block to stake your claim in the hereafter. The American consumers will adore you. They'll beat a path to your door.

Of course, if they should happen to be disappointed at your door you might end up like the old codger being ridden out of town on a rail. As he wiped the tar and feathers out of his eyes he was heard to say, "If it weren't for the honor of it all, I'd just as soon have walked."

Dear Andy:

Sometimes I begin to wonder whether the system has gotten to be too much for anyone to cope with. Here I am now, president of my company. It has taken thirty-two years, but I finally made it. Time to begin to enjoy some of the fruits of the struggle? Hardly. If anything, my newly won status and financial position make life more difficult than ever.

Take my home life. Besides my wife there are two teen-age tyrants who live there. The boy is eighteen, the girl is nineteen. They are my legal children by birth but not, they indicate, by choice. Like the night I first announced at the dinner table that I had been elected president. You might have expected a shout of glee, a congratulatory hug, or at least a friendly nod. Not at my address. Instead the male child said, "I suppose we're going to move now to a more expensive neighborhood to show how important you are," and the female offspring said, "I wonder how many more underprivileged blacks and hillbillies will have to slave in the fields to bring in all that extra money the company will be giving you."

In short order I was informed by them that buying a bigger house, a fancier car, sable coats, groomed poodles, and sundry pieces of jewelry were definitely not to take place. Conspicuous consumption is the sure sign of a decaying society and they could not possibly hold their heads up with their friends if their parents showed up so troglodyte. As a matter of fact, they said, they had made concessions enough for my image by agreeing to go to those lousy big name Ivy League trade schools.

The male of the two then proceeded to lecture me on the evils of that arch symbol of decadent status: the country club. Thank God religion is dying, he said; now if only the country club could go the way of the atrophying Greek letter fraternities maybe the privileged would be forced out of their sanctuaries to face up to their responsibilities in the real world.

All that I strived for years to achieve—a good education for my kids, a bit of recognition for business achievement, some of the comforts of life in the company of gracious, well-mannered people, a few luxuries that are the reward of rank —are like ashes now in my hands. The more I get the heavier the pall that descends on my house. Even my wife feels uneasy and guilty now about the luxuries we can afford.

On the other hand, in the office I have to cope with a situation at the other extreme. The chairman told me the other day that it would not do for the president of the company to be riding the commuter train any more. From now on a chauffered limousine would pick me up every morning and bring me home at night, as befits the operating head of a company of our importance. The first day the car arrived I was so embarrassed in front of my family that I got in up front with the uniformed driver. I well knew the comments I would get from my young activists when I got home that night. And for that I even had to give up my friendly train bridge game, perhaps forever.

A few days ago my secretary told me she has heard via the office grapevine that there was a ground swell of grumbling among the vice presidents about the personal car I own. It seems my Buick does not allow enough room for the lower echelons to buy what they consider decent model cars. Because it would be unseemly for them to own cars better than or even equal to the president's, they now have to scale themselves down from medium-size Oldsmobiles, Pontiacs, or Mercurys. And *their* subordinates will, in turn, be restricted to the Chevrolet-Ford-Plymouth level. All this motor squeeze could be eased by my trading in the Buick for an El Dorado or a big Lincoln Continental. I started secretly looking at new cars this weekend, but I don't know how I can bring one home.

I happen to live in a nice town in Connecticut. But our house is on the small side. The maid's room, for instance, is too near the downstairs recreation area and late parties tend to keep her up. So we have been considering for some time a move to a bit more gracious place. But we haven't yet figured out how to work it out with our kids. I was quite startled by the bold suggestion of one of the company's board members, whom I know quite well. He flat out told me that this is now a good time to buy a place in the estate section of Greenwich. The man is a banker and he knows quite well that with tight mortgage money and skyrocketing prices in Greenwich this is one of the *worst* times to buy. I said so to him, and he looked at me as if I were crazy. "It is not a matter of general economic conditions," he said. "It is simply that you cannot afford *not* to move in your present position. The cost of money should be your *last* consideration."

And that's how it goes. Caught between Scylla and Charybdis, the nut and the cracker. Whichever way I turn I am sure to lose. Is there No Exit?

Sincerely,
Sorely Tried

Dear Sorely Tried:

You are truly a victim of your success, living proof that the American Dream fulfilled can be a veritable nightmare.

Perhaps you have only one recourse remaining. In one bold stroke you could martyr yourself in your children's eyes as you make your ultimate statement on the condition of our society, while at the same time protesting the high-level chickenshit in your company so that future presidents may have a freer hand to move and act as they will.

But if you do commit suicide, don't be too showy about it.

Dear Andy:

Company parties have always bored me. The people wear their best masks and tiptoe through their ritualized dances, speaking safe comments about suburban life situations, problems with schools, the indecencies of Con Edison, the iniquities of the Telephone Company, and the manifold indignities caused by the various commuter railroads.

I decided that this time the dinner party for the top managers of my division and their wives would be different. For once the people would really get to *know* each other, not just see the confected surfaces and hear the synchronized sounds. Because I particularly wanted to get to know my men's wives better and to learn something of their particular life styles, I hit upon a nice little psychological game for us all to play. Shortly after the last liqueur had been quaffed and all seven couples had left the dining room, I introduced the game.

In order for it to work, I explained, everybody must take his or her directions seriously. At the end of each round we would vote who was the most honest, and that person would be exempt from the ensuing rounds. The grand loser would be penalized by having to leave the party immediately and go home alone. That disgrace should provide sufficient incentive. The first round of the game was for wives only.

I heard a few muffled moans and gasps, but no more than I expected. As I looked at the faces of the men I saw almost uniformly pained consternation. You would have thought they were about to enter a chamber of horrors.

I brought out a pack of cards, which I had numbered, with one direction printed on each card. Each direction was designed to expose certain inner beliefs and dispositions of the player. I explained that whoever picked the card numbered 1 would be the first to perform, during which we would all take notes. Then number 2 would go, etc. At the end of the round all of us, men and women alike, would vote.

I passed out the cards face down to each of the wives, including my own. One woman read hers and promptly fainted. She had drawn the card stating "Show in pantomime just what your husband really thinks of each of the men in the room." Fortunately, she was scheduled to be fifth in line, so there was time to revive her and let her regain her composure.

My wife, to whom this part of the party was just as much a surprise as it was to the others, muttered *sotto voce* an extraordinarily vulgar expression for a Wellesley girl whose father was a deacon, when she saw her card was: "Demonstrate how you think each of the women in this room caught her husband."

Despite the initial general hostility, I think the game would have gone off pretty well if it had not been for the unfortunate piece of luck in that poor Mrs. Caldwell, the wife of the budgetary control manager, drew the number 1 card. Then, too, if she had gotten one of the other cards, such as: "Demonstrate the prime way in which your husband is a phony," or "If you had it to do all over again how would you direct your husband's career?" she might have been able to cope. But she drew the card stating: "Tell why you do not think you belong here tonight."

She was a wispy little character with washed-out features and shifty eyes that never looked you straight in the face. She started out by saying she did not understand the direction, did not understand the game, did not know why she was here tonight anyway. Then she began to weep. She said she was a millstone around her husband's neck, she had two children but did not deserve them, and that she had never finished college and couldn't understand her husband's work. I looked over at Caldwell, her husband, to see what he thought of all this. He was staring blankly at the floor between his feet. Meanwhile, his wife had now begun discussing why she had been undergoing analysis for the past three years, how that was the only reason Caldwell had not yet divorced her, and that she knew it was her fault that her older daughter was a hopeless drug addict.

I thought Mrs. Caldwell had rather overly caught the spirit of the game and she would make it too difficult an act for the others to follow, so I tried to get her to stop. I made one remark which she did not seem to hear, and as I approached her repeating the admonition to cease, she whirled on me and threw the contents of her highball in my face. She then ran screaming from the room.

Caldwell, without even apologizing to me for her actions, rushed out after her.

Needless to say, that bit of exhibitionism ended the game. A few moments later someone remembered a baby-sitter with an early curfew, and soon they all found excuses to leave. It was the earliest ending to any dinner party we had ever given.

In the days that followed I found Caldwell's work began to deteriorate badly. He was often late with his budgets, and his explanations were wretched. I spoke with him about it and he tried to alibi by explaining that now that his wife had had to be institutionalized he was further burdened by having additional problems with his children. Finally, just the other day Caldwell submitted a budget analysis that was so ill-conceived as to be virtually seditious. I must take some severe disciplinary action with him or run the personal risk of invidious comparison with other successful division managers in the company. But if I do there will be many of my managerial staff, especially those who attended the party, who will deplore the action on aimlessly soft humanistic grounds. Yet I need these people working in harmony with me.

Thus do we paint ourselves into corners in our quest for knowledge and understanding. What is your thought as to my next action?

[Signed] *Concerned*

Dear Concerned:

Your preoccupation with your staff may be affecting your personality. What you really need is a proper diversion or hobby. There is a cute little shop downtown that caters to just the kind of amusements to fit your needs. The whips come in several sizes and in various shades of blood, and the chains are all suitably gnarled and rusted for more satisfying impressions. Just knock twice and ask for the owner, Mark de Sade. He'll be more than willing to demonstrate the toys, though you may very well be able to teach *him* a thing or two.

10 / Bridging the Information Gap

"IT IS FOR EACH MAN," SAID A NINETEENTH-CENTURY French philosopher, "to procure himself the morality which suits him."

In the world of business today it is sometimes difficult to determine if the accent is on *morality* or on *procuring*. Perhaps this is because the rules of the game are inadequately drawn, thus favoring those with the most flexible consciences.

There is one particular area where such flexibility is becoming rampant. Because so great a premium is often placed on critical information, the practice of industrial espionage is enjoying an almost incredible boom. Indeed, some astute observers predict that at the current rate of growth it may be only another few years before the gathering of intelligence as currently pursued by governments in military and diplomatic affairs will become a commonly recognized function in American industrial corporations.

It is quite conceivable that someday formal departments of Competitive Knowledge will be established, headed by corporate officers. Men with CIA or FBI training will be much sought after in business, just as airlines seek retired Air Force pilots today. And an understanding of the detection uses of the most sophisticated technologies, from computers through laser beams and earth-girdling satellites, will be a basic qualification for employment.

Though this may very well be the direction in which

business information-seeking is headed, it remains a fact that industrial spying, bribing, and extortion are still twilight activities that are often covered by civil and criminal laws. Therefore, what sort of intelligence can be so vital nowadays as to cause normally conservative, God-fearing, law-abiding businessmen not only to bend their consciences but also to risk exposure and prosecution?

Heading the list is inside information that can be useful in an effort to take over a company from the outside. Specifically in demand are stockholder records, especially the names and addresses of the company's largest holders; the company's emergency counter-takeover plan along with its privately acknowledged weaknesses; and details of dubious activities on the part of principal officers of the firm that could make lurid reading for the stockholders. This type of information can be critical, and substantial sums have been expended in rather ingenious ways to obtain it.

The easiest, though not always the cheapest method, is the direct payment to a disgruntled employee, someone who may even be high up— but not as high as he feels he should be—on the executive ladder. Often this someone will make himself known to the raider and seek to make a deal. The deal may involve payment in money or promise of improved status, or both. Frequently a throw-in on the deal is the promise to chop one or two individuals meticulously selected by the informer. This throw-in might actually be the prime motivation. Where such inside information vendors are not readily available, more circuitous and time-consuming methods have been used. The planted employee was a favorite device back in the days when the major emphasis of industrial espionage was on the pilfering of trade secrets, formulas, and production techniques. This method is still in vogue for certain types of long-range espionage, but the great amount of time it requires to position the "feeder" renders it rather impractical in a takeover situation.

Secretaries and wives may be prime imformation sources if strategically selected and properly cultivated. Vanity, avarice, jealousy, concupiscence, envy, and even good old-fashioned hatred can be helpful triggers to the act of shooting off the mouth. Sometimes the chairman's secretary or the executive vice president's wife requires a little special help to get her vocal cords lubricated. This, too, can be arranged. Some off-duty actors and male models have developed flourishing cottage industries for just this type of service.

When the target individuals do not succumb to these rather genteel methods or when the time budget is so short as to require faster results, a more straightforward technique may be employed. Skilled historical researchers are engaged to do a crash job of developing a dossier of the person's most vulnerable points. Favorite items in this quest for knowledge: secret mistresses, long-buried police records, falsified expense or tax reports, and past homosexual experiences. Naturally, photographs or microfilms are sought, but well-documented hearsay will often serve the purpose.

With this kind of graphic personal data in hand it is only a short step for the impatient corporate information seeker to effect a trade for what he wants from the now vincible character. Though mutual threats of violence and charges of blackmail often accompany the confrontation, this system of accumulating knowledge continues to prove as efficient as any.

Recently, one type of firm that specializes in interpersonal relationships has developed a sideline of intelligence gathering. Certain executive search firms which customarily accept assignments to find qualified men for important industrial posts have found that they can earn even higher fees by finding out certain desired information.

This is the way they do it. The headhunter calls in a strategic executive with the target company and discusses a potential (wholly fictitious) job opportunity with another company at a salary much above his current rate. To determine the candidate's qualifications, the headhunter asks him a number of questions. The flattered executive often spills everything he knows in an effort to show how important he is. The man from the search firm acts, of course, duly impressed. Several such conversations with key executives of

the target company usually enables the headhunter's client to piece together the information it requires.

This type of knowledge-seeking is by no means exclusively confined to the attackers. Often a besieged company will resort to espionage in order to prepare an effective defense. Who is behind the purchases of big blocks of its stock is usually a subject of more than mild curiosity. Usually the purchases are made in "Street names"—that is, fictitious names confected by brokers for clients who do not want their identity revealed. But some clerk in the broker's back office has to handle the deal. Knowing precisely who that clerk is and knowing what it will take to get him to talk has become a special art perfected by certain proxy solicitors, law firms, and fund managers. The trick is to locate the right firm with the special talent. That in itself takes a certain kind of talent, but it is available.

It is said that if you want to learn something badly enough and are willing to pay enough, there is virtually nothing today that can be kept secret from you. Since informers cannot always be found (or created), some of our finest scientific minds have managed to extend the horizons of knowledge-gathering by putting their electronic learning into utilitarian forms.

One of the country's top authorities in the use of wiretaps, bugs, and detectors admits that less than 1 percent of the bugs and taps are ever discovered. For the simple fact is the art of detection has lagged far behind the technology of information-gathering. There is one interesting little eavesdropping aid with coast-to-coast range. Sometimes referred to as the infinity transmitter, this high-powered device converts an ordinary telephone into a microphone that picks up and transmits all the conversation in a room. Once the phone has been bugged, the ardent researcher merely dials the number from some distant location and then, before the phone rings, he blows a whistle into his own phone. The tone turns on the transmitter in the bugged instrument and prevents the phone from ringing. The bugged phone acts as a broadcaster as long as it stays in the cradle. Only lifting the receiver can break the connection. This little device is made to order for modern direct-dial service. Other gear designed to record important conversations are a voice-actuated miniature transistor that can be tucked into a book binding; a fountain pen transmitter; and a James Bond-ish electronic spike for martini olives, perfect for plugging in on convivial blabbermouths.

If a bugging device should happen to be discovered, the advantage passes to the discoverer. With a bit of self-control and creative imagination, he can stage some meetings exclusively for the benefit of the transmitter and the fascinated spy on the other end. Handled with taste and restraint he could well lead the eavesdropper down an endless garden path.

Technicians hired to debug offices are not always completely trustworthy. Some have been known to accept fees to debug offices that they were previously paid by someone else to bug. Thus they collect fees two ways. Others are not above selling information about their client to the target after they have completed their original bugging assignment.

But in the main these electronic operatives (a great many of whom like to boast of experience with the FBI) are reasonably trustworthy in a thoroughly deceitful line of work. They, too, have their occasional triumphs which they are fond of relating to prospective clients. Like the time this particular private eye was called down to South Carolina to the plantation of a famous aging tycoon. The tycoon was concerned about movements in the price of the stock of the company of which he was chairman and principal stock-holder. The company directors were discussing plans to make a tender offer for some of the company's own stock and it was essential that none of that information leak out, especially the proposed tender price. Well, our faithful shamus brought all his electronic detecting paraphernalia plus two assistants with him down to the plantation. He determined that most business discussions customarily took place in the large paneled study. His equipment indicated the presence there of some sort of device, and so he and his troops went about the room combing and sifting everything they touched. Meanwhile, the tycoon sat there watching television. Hours went by with no success in locating the bug. Then, fortunately, the tycoon got up to leave the room. He snapped off the TV set and suddenly the detecting equipment needle began to hemorrhage. And so it dawned: in the TV set itself. Upon dismantling the set the detective discovered a pinhead microphone wired to the on-off switch. When the set was switched on, the microphone went off. When the set was switched off, the mike went on. The spy had obviously operated on the theory that no important discussions would be held while the TV set was on, but serious time would come when the set was off. Further investigation turned up the fact that six weeks earlier the TV set had been removed from the house for two or three days for repairs at a local shop. It had been fixed in more ways than one.

Still, it is not always possible for the electronic sneaks to get in and plant their little devices. Faced with that sort of impasse, the insistent interloper may accomplish his purpose with a long-range zoom-lensed camera that can be stationed miles away from the target company's office. All he needs is a clear shot at the window where he knows the key conferences are held. He can then film the meetings on high-speed videotape and later bring in a professional lipreader to read the filmed conversation.

Cameras play a large role in industry's seeking of information. Just as microphones have been designed down to the size of a pinhead and amplifiers to virtually the same dimension, cameras can now be made the size of a button. A decade ago Gary Powers and his U-2 spy plane downed over Russia made headline news. Less well known is the fact that some automobile companies have been sending their own spy planes over their competitors' proving grounds for years with nary a shot fired at them in anger. They are really gentlemen out there in Detroit.

But science marches on, and today's spy has at his disposal lasers, sonic spectrums, cesium transmitters that can aim sound-carrying light waves at the sky and bounce them off the ionosphere to a receiver miles away, and contraptions to transmit pictures via satellite and via sound through the earth's crust and through water.

Remember, too, this is the era of the computer and much important corporate information is stored in data banks. A simple phone tap by a modern hawkshaw can determine where the corporation leases time; then after the access code is secured a tap on that computer bank can gain in minutes the results of millions of dollars of research. A typical corporate computer center is poorly guarded and presents an easy mark for the practical spy. Sometimes detailed stockholder lists are on computers at the company's transfer agent bank. The unsuspecting clerk who works with the machine at the bank usually presents no great problem to the indefatigable seeker. A tape with fifty million characters can be copied in a few minutes without leaving a trace.

Yes, an efficient espionage crew can do a great deal for a company's profitability. It can discover chemical formulas without expensive, time-consuming laboratory research. It can determine a competitor's marketing plans for a new product and enable the company to foul up the competitor's tests so that they can never get an accurate line on their product's strengths and weaknesses. A good spy corps can ascertain a rival's bid for an important contract so that the company can enter a slightly lower bid to win the sealed auction. It can solve problems on which dozens of somebody else's scientists and engineers have been working for years.

With the current squeeze on capital expenditures, many more companies may be turning to this shortcut to self-improvement. Even some of the older forms of prying and lying are making a comeback. Lockpickers, who have been dawdling for years, are at present commanding $200 to $300 per week in Manhattan for practicing their specialty. And now there is talk of a coming boom in forgers and counterfeiters in view of all the confusion in brokerage house back offices.

11 / The Strategists

IT WAS 5:40 P.M. ON A COLD, WINTRY DAY IN NEW YORK. Most of the offices uptown were well on their way to emptying. Down among the Wall Street canyons the general depeopling process had started even earlier in the day. But at the law office of Hendricks, Stuffwell & Longdale at least three conference rooms on three separate floors were just beginning to accumulate the people destined to confer late into the night in scenes of great tension and creative scheming.

Stuffwell himself was sitting in on the most important of these meetings—the one in the twenty-second-floor boardroom. Clarence Stuffwell, at seventy-three, was the senior partner of Hendricks, Stuffwell, a firm founded more than a half century ago by his venerated father, former Supreme Court Justice Cyrus Stuffwell, and John Hutley Hendricks, former Secretary of War under President Wilson. The third name partner, F. Tucker Longdale, had been a well-endowed and very well connected member of a very socially prominent New York and Bar Harbor family. Though not renowned for his legal mind, Longdale had earned one of the most discreetly libidinous reputations in all of high society. Many currently successful Wall Streeters suspect a touch of Longdale in their family tree. While all three name partners are deceased, the tradition-encrusted corporate law firm they founded now has over 150 lawyers and is generally regarded as one of the eight or ten largest and most prestigious law firms in the country.

It was a rare case that could intrigue Mr. Clarence Stuffwell to the extent that he was willing to spend a whole evening in town with it. For Stuffwell, as his acolyte and doorknob turner, Waldo Craven, often said, "had seen it all and done it all." But the effort to save the giant Kansas City-based Basic International Foodstuffs, Inc. from the grasp of sly Ephraim Rader was sufficient to de-jade even Stuffwell.

Basic International Foodstuffs, Inc. is a billion-dollar-sales-per-year food manufacturing company, which makes and distributes hot and cold cereals for man and beast all over the world. In its sixty-six years of existence it has grown from a Midwestern wheat, corn, and rye processor to one of the most widely multinational companies on the globe. Indeed, more than 60 percent of its profits now come from nations outside the United States, and in addition to various industrial and consumer cereals it makes and sells cake mixes, coffee, tea, canned fruits and vegetables. But it drifted late onto the convenience food tide of the past two decades, missed entirely the TV and snack food craze of the last decade, and has seen the positions of many of its formerly market-leading grocery products at home gradually erode to where it now has a collection of second- and third-rated, though high-quality, brands. Its plants around the world are for the most part overly large and relatively inefficient, and its sales force is long on experience and short on sideburns. BIF, which has not missed a dividend for fifty-eight years and is still classified as a blue chip by Standard & Poor and the Chase Manhattan's trust department, is an overripe pear. Ephraim Rader, who has resuscitated a railroad, a box-maker, and a meat-packer in recent years, apparently feels he knows just the fruit salad to accommodate it.

Seated now at the head of his magnificent banded rosewood oval conference table, the tall, stately Stuffwell coughed delicately once or twice to signify he was about to call the meeting to order. Before the ideas begin to flow, let us quickly run around the table to identify the actors in this high corporate drama.

At Stuffwell's immediate right, crouched head down and pencil poised over a yellow legal-size pad, was the aforementioned Waldo Craven, a pinched old man at thirty-two but ever alert to catch the shadings of Stuffwell's expositions. His formal legal training is impeccable, but his associates regard his sole contributions to be strictly clerical and Stuffwell-amplification, in that order of importance.

Moving counterclockwise around the table, next to Craven is Manny Oxenberg, short, very stout, and resplendent in his gold-green iridescent suit. He is puffing on a long, dark cigar now and staring meditatively at the opposite wall. Oxenberg is one of the very few top proxy law specialists in the country, and he has been retained here as much to prevent Ephraim Rader from retaining him as to help plot the defense strategy for BIF. Oxenberg's knowledge of personalities at the SEC and what they will and will not clear in the way of communications and tactics in a takeover situation is far more accurate than that of the entire Stuffwell law firm. That, plus his precise knowledge of the law and his reputation for devilish cleverness in tender attacks and proxy defenses, makes him one of the main characters in this evening's action.

Alongside Oxenberg is his frequent co-conspirator, the burly, mustachioed Jim Robbe. Robbe is a schemer for all seasons. He heads a proxy soliciting firm, considers himself an expert communicator, master financial strategist, public opinion pulse-taker *sine qua non,* and no mean legal tactician of the visceral rather than book-learnin' variety. He has been the last to arrive this evening, having rushed over from another strategy session at a nervous company headquarters a few blocks away.

Continuing counterclockwise, next to Robbe sit two vice presidents of Basic International Foodstuffs. Since they will have very little of distinction to say during the course of the meeting, we shall identify them only as Smith I and Smith II. The evening will be an education for them.

At the foot of the table, looking tense but coolly controlled as he traces intricate geometric doodles on the pad in front of him, is Richard Anderson, the executive vice president and chief operating officer of BIF. He is the client.

To Anderson's right is Alan Burnham, the corporate secretary of BIF, the man with all the company's stockholder records and financial data in his briefcase. He is also the primary company liaison with the legal talent and was responsible for retaining the Hendricks, Stuffwell firm as well as Oxenberg, the individual operator.

Next to Burnham is Frank Quigley, the veteran public relations counselor who was once a business news columnist for a now-defunct New York newspaper. In the last couple of years he has been on the opposite side writing stockholder letters, news releases, and ads to help the defense against many an Oxenberg-masterminded attack, but he is rather pleased to be playing this time on the same team as that "tricky little son of a bitch." However, being forced to listen to that uncouth blowhard, Jim Robbe, Oxenberg's frequent cohort and once again collaborator, bids fair to take all the fun out of the occasion for Quigley.

Sitting next to him is Scott Winterpenny, one of the brightest junior partners of Hendricks, Stuffwell. He is an experienced merger attorney, who has also recorded considerable government combat time after his early sentence at the *Yale Law Review*.

To his right is another of the major characters of this evening's drama: L. Stuart LaCroix. Gray-haired, gray-faced, he looks like all joy has long since been drained from his body. He is one of the senior partners of the powerful international investment banking firm of the House of Vehl, and it is expected that he will be the bearer of a vital piece of news to this gathering of eagles this evening.

LaCroix's assistant, John Cipher, sits beside him fussing with some heavily benumbered papers in a worn, though elegant, Mark Cross attaché case.

His throat cleared, Stuffwell began to sputter. He spent several minutes commenting on the weather (which was quite ordinary for this time of year) and thanking them all for coming here this evening (as if they could easily have chosen to honor any one of several cocktail parties or cotillions instead of coming to his humble digs). He then delivered a totally unnecessary summary of the situation to date, reminding them all that Ephraim Rader had registered with the SEC a holding of 2.1 million shares or approximately 17 percent of BIF's outstanding common stock, that tight money conditions made it unlikely that he would try to gain more stock through a cash tender offer, and that the recent drop in the price of Rader's company stock made it almost as certain he could not effectively launch an equity or convertible debenture paper exchange offer for BIF stock. What was left was Rader's only course if BIF management continued to refuse to merge with him—a proxy fight. With the BIF annual stockholder meeting scheduled for mid-April, only three months away, this stacked up now as a virtual certainty.

"Why even speculate on it?" Robbe said. "I happen to know that Rader has already retained two proxy soliciting firms. He approached me first, undoubtedly hoping to at least sterilize me so I wouldn't be fighting him."

"So that is established," Stuffwell said. "Clearly we must come out of this meeting tonight with a viable plan of defense."

"With clear assignments for everybody," said Craven the echo.

"Mr. LaCroix," said Stuffwell, "I understand you have been in touch with people abroad. Have you anything to report now to the group?"

The House of Vehl partner frowned, and without seeming to move his pallid lips said, "In an hour we shall put through a phone call to my principal in Rio de Janeiro. After that I can give you the definitive word. But first I must have an answer to the key question he will ask. What will be our argument against Rader's primary line of attack in the proxy contest?"

"And what exactly do you think that attack will be?" said Stuffwell.

"Nine consecutive quarters of flat or declining earnings, a cut in dividend, no new product lines introduced in five years except a predigested senior citizens gourmet food line that laid the biggest and most expensive egg since the Edsel . . . must I go on? In short, incompetent management." LaCroix's investment banking eyes narrowed. "I hate to be so blunt, but we're talking in terms of many millions of dollars. My principal needs some assurances."

"What kind of assurances are required, sir?" Richard Anderson, the tall, young executive vice president of BIF spoke up in a firm, well-modulated voice. Midwesternese, according to that great language expert H. L. Mencken, is the most virile speech spoken in this country. Anderson, his crew cut graying slightly at the temples and clad in a loose-fitting dark blue suit with blue and red striped tie, looked as if he could run back out onto the basketball court at Northwestern tomorrow, and he sounded as if he would count cadence for the team's exercise first.

LaCroix turned to Stuffwell. "I think perhaps a few of us should have a short caucus outside before we go on."

At this point, Manny Oxenberg, who had been languidly picking his nose, started to talk. The accent was south Bronx, but the delivery would not have disgraced Clarence Darrow. "Let's not kid ourselves or waste our time. This company is in deep trouble. We're all big boys here and we can face the facts. There are 30,000 damned unhappy stockholders who've seen BIF stock go from 73 to 24 in less than two years. No other major food company has dropped so sharply, even in this bear market. Ephraim

Rader is now by far your biggest single stockholder with 17 percent of the stock. He has a record of success in revitalizing sick companies. Twenty percent more of BIF's stock is held by funds. I'd worry about where that might go. The 15 percent held by bank trust departments could be a problem, too. Rader's got a lot of guns to take into a proxy contest. We've got to be able to convince most of the little stockholders not to vote for him. To do that we've got to take some of his best arguments away from him. This is what Mr. LaCroix is getting at. Frankly, we must show the stockholders that the very same changes that Rader will say he'll make are *already* being made."

"How can we do that?" Anderson said.

"By starting off with a change in top management," Jim Robbe, the proxy solicitor, interjected. "Defending the records of those two old fogies sitting as chairman and president will be as effective as Betty Crocker defending her honor at a longshoremen's stag party. What is she going to say, 'Keep your lousy hands off my cookies'? She has no right to be there in the first place."

Silence fell on the room. Score six points for the dead-end kids, Quigley the PR man thought. They got through the corncob wall. Now that that's stripped away, we'll start working around the bone.

But Stuffwell felt called upon then to relieve the tension. "Perhaps we should order sandwiches sent in. We're likely to be here for some time yet. Waldo, will you take the orders? Gentlemen, if you would like olives, pickles, or mayonnaise please so indicate."

Omigod, thought Quigley, at a billing rate of maybe four hundred dollars an hour he's a frustrated short-order clerk.

Craven performed his assignment efficiently and the orders were quickly taken and he left. Scott Winterpenny assumed the chore of taking notes on the meeting while Craven was gone.

Quigley thought he could start earning his fee by getting the meeting back on the track, so he commented that while Robbe was undoubtedly speaking from the standpoint of the difficulty of soliciting proxies out in the boondocks, he himself could speak of the need for a series of telling points to be made in the *letters* to the stockholders. "We've got to give them something, some indication of a better future so we can say that Rader is trying to steal their birthright for himself."

Burnham, the BIF corporate secretary, who until now had done nothing at the meeting but puff away on his curved bowl pipe, broke his spell apologetically. "Dick," he said to Anderson, "I think these gentlemen ought to know that Mr. Venneman and Mr. Mahoney, our chairman and president, are planning to retire after the annual meeting."

"Well, that's an interesting piece of news," Stuffwell said.

"That's a break," Robbe said.

"Dick Anderson will be our next president," Burnham said.

Anderson smiled shyly.

"Why wait till the annual meeting?" Oxenberg said. "It may be too late by then. Announce it now so you can start building a record in the next few weeks. Close obsolete plants, cut costs, buy a company or two, shift around a few divisions. Consolidate, economize, innovate. Get it going now so we can point to it in the next couple of months."

"I cannot ask Mr. Venneman and Mr. Mahoney to tender their resignations now," Anderson said. "It would be humiliating to them. It would look like they were admitting to being responsible for BIF's decline."

"Exactly! Listen," said Oxenberg, his temper rising,

"this is no nursery school play. The only good those two guys can do for the company now is to get out fast before Rader gets in and cans them. If they want to give you a chance to turn this company around they first of all have got to help you hold the job. You won't hold the job, you won't beat off Rader, unless you can make it look like you're breaking cleanly with them and are moving decisively to improve the company. They are losers. Their record proves it. No matter how nice they are, how gentle and sweet, how much they give to charity and help little old ladies cross in traffic, they are responsible for having run the company down. They lost stockholders' money. That's all that counts in this game. That's the biggest crime. You are part of it unless you can make it clear that you are working with a fresh deck of cards in behalf of the stockholders. All our strategy has to be built around the new broom theme *here now*. You doing *now* what Rader can only *promise* to do."

Anderson looked at Burnham, who puffed meditatively on his pipe. Anderson looked at Smith I and Smith II, and they lowered their eyes. He knew he was alone in this den of friends.

LaCroix dotted the i and crossed the t. "If I could indicate to my principal in Rio that the top executive positions are about to be changed and sweeping new management moves are in the works," he said, "I believe he would see his way clear to move immediately on the preferred issue we've discussed."

The "preferred" issue was a proposed sale of 250,000 new convertible preferred stock with five votes per share and a conversion right to five shares of BIF common stock each. The new preferred stock would be priced at $120 a share and carry an 8 percent dividend. Basic International

Foodstuff's common stock was then selling at around $25 per share, giving the deal an extra little inducement. When converted this would put the equivalent of 1.25 million shares in friendly hands and not only substantially counterbalance Rader's 2.1 million shares but reduce his percentage ownership from 17 percent to 15 percent.

"Of course, no stockholder approval is necessary for the sale of the preferred stock because it has been previously authorized and the total to be issued is convertible at less than 18 percent of outstanding shares," said Winterpenny to Oxenberg. "But is there a chance that the preferred alone could block any merger on a class basis even if Rader should one day get 51 percent of the common?"

"There's a chance, but not much because he'd sue us for specifically setting this up, and he'd probably be able to make it stick in court because of anticipation of a proxy fight," Oxenberg said. "But if we get the preferred placed properly, that will make it 10 percent for our side. Add the 5 percent holdings of company officers and directors, 10 percent from the banks who don't like to vote for raiders if they can keep out of fiduciary trouble, and you have 25 percent. Ten percent of the little old lady stockholders from Des Moines to Dallas constitutionally could not vote against management if they heard it straight from Luther and the Pope. That could be worth 300,000 votes for our side. We may buy another company for stock, and that will give us a few hundred thousand more. Maybe we'll only have to pick up another 20 percent. We'll get that with a good story of new vital, dynamic management action and a little casting of doubt on Rader's true motives—greed, avarice, chicanery—in seeking to force this merger. Along with, of course, the kind of doorbell-ringing, proxy-soliciting campaign that only Jim Robbe can organize."

Robbe gave his cohort his best Aw-shucks-it's-only-routine look, and Quigley had to turn away to keep from gagging.

"Don't forget the antitrust action we're working on," Winterpenny said. "We won't win it, but it can tie him up for a few months. At today's cost of money that will be a little tight cheese, too."

"All right," Anderson said decisively. "This is what I'll do. I'll fly back to Kansas City tonight and see Mr. Venneman and Mr. Mahoney the first thing tomorrow. If they don't go along with our plan, I shall resign."

Smith I looked at Smith II and a wispy, knowing smile creased the lips of first one then the other.

"Good, that's settled," said Stuffwell. "Here are our sandwiches now. Dig in, folks. We've got a lot of work ahead of us tonight. Should we put in that call to Rio now?"

12 / The Tragic Tale of a Comic Conglomerator

LAST YEAR HE WAS THE SCOURGE OF THE STREET. A TRIPLE threat—manager, money-raiser, market manipulator—and he could do no wrong. Seemingly overnight, Haight Harvey Hale had burst forth as one of the two or three most spectacular of all the new multi-company Machiavellis. His vehicle, HHH Industries, had shot up to 170 on the Amex with a peak price-earnings ratio of 95. Hale's more than one-million-share holding put his personal fortune at close to a quarter-billion dollars.

The *New Yorker* profiled him. *Life* showed him at play with his third wife and four Dobermans. The *New York Times* did a Sunday feature analyzing his audacious use of debt financing. *Time* and *Forbes* did cover stories and *Playboy* had J. Paul Getty philosophize about how his meteoric saga was possible only in America. One syndicated women's columnist even did a piece on his solution to ending the Vietnam War ("Send in the SDS and the Chicago police; let the winner take all"). Haight Hale, instant legend at twenty-nine.

But that was a year ago. Today, following four consecutive quarters of sharply dropping earnings, HHH Industries' stock stands at 13. It is in the vanguard of the most dramatic declines-of-the-year lists. Five major stockholder suits against him are now vying for court time. Hale's socialite wife has left him, and several key executives have left his company. So many little old ladies in tennis shoes have tried to attack him that Hale has unlisted phone numbers, an electrified wire fence, and round-the-clock bodyguards. On the Street he has become one of the preeminent members of a small, sad group known as the comic conglomerators. Where once there was awe, now there is only derision.

We look in on young Mr. Hale now as he sits in his Park Avenue office furiously pedaling his Exercycle. His trusted old (thirty-seven) comptroller, Fairweather, speaks.

"Why must you always do that? Is it some form of self-flagellation?"

"It's one way of keeping in shape," said Hale. "Healthy body, healthy mind. I've got to keep my stamina up to outlast this damn tight money market. Last night I played three hours of squash at the Yale Club."

"I didn't know you'd gone to Yale."

"I didn't. I went to CCNY, but I have an arrangement."

"Well, do me a favor and try to stop pedaling for a moment and prepare yourself for the meeting. The prince will be here in a few minutes."

"I have nothing to prepare. My mind is made up. That man has got to go. He's bleeding us white. Cosmetics stocks led the market on the upside last year with an average 30 percent rise, but our masterpiece was our biggest losing subsidiary. We're being powder-puffed to death."

"Maybe we can sell it," said Fairweather.

"Exactly. We'll divest ourselves of a nonfitting, though valuable, property. And with the proceeds we'll retire some of that debt that's killing us. But first we'll have to get rid of the prince. Nobody'll touch that company with him around."

"What will you do with it if you can't sell it?"

"Hell, I could liquidate it and we'd be better off than

we are now. But I'm sure I can peddle it. Meanwhile, I'll run the outfit myself."

"How are you going to break the news to the prince?" said Fairweather. "It's an operation he built from the ground up. He's an emotional Hungarian. He might do something drastic."

"He's had plenty of time to do something drastic to that *operation*. I made a grave mistake relying on him. It

may even have been a mistake to have even gotten into the cosmetics business. It's too personal a business to run scientifically. You must have a strong, creative, with-it personality running it and extending his psyche through every lipstick case and spray can. Like Revson or Rubenstein."

"Maybe it's our corporate organization that's at fault, too," said Fairweather. "We gave him too little supervision. We had too few financial controls and management reviews. All we gave him were sales and earnings goals. We gave him no technical or marketing support. He gained nothing in his alliance with us and was actually hurt in at least two important ways. His customers lost some respect for him, for they felt he was no longer his own man. And he was forced into more of an administrative role, something he does very poorly. I tell you, Haight, he's got some valid arguments if he knows how to make them. But you really dislike him personally underneath it all."

"False. He has no argument and the decision was made on a purely scientific basis. Personality never entered."

"I just hope he doesn't go berserk like that other one," said Fairweather. "Otto Grosz-Esel. Otto and his magic computer leasing company. When you squeezed him out with that bank maneuver . . ."

"Consummate purity. He was the kind who would always overextend himself."

"Yes, but I well remember that scene at Le Pavillon when Otto realized what had happened to him and how he registered his appreciation. He tried to slice you with his steak knife."

Hale stopped pedaling. "Otto was insane," he said. "Crazy Otto, we used to call him. The prince, on the other hand, is just nutty. He has delusions of adequacy. His problem, and ours, is that he has lost touch with his

market. Even *he* must realize that now. That last spray cologne he brought out—Detached Retina, 'for the gal who
wants to knock his eye out'—that's too much."

"My sister bought some and she says it works."

"On linebackers and stevedores. That stuff is so heavy
it pollutes the air."

"All right. But this sudden firing will further your
image of ruthlessness unless you have some humane plan
for him."

"What's happening to you, Fairweather? You used to
look at numbers and see cash flow. You used to look at
plants and see production. Now all you see is poor people
and pain and suffering. Are you practicing to be a sociolo-
gist?"

"I'm a realist. Morale in our company is shot. Everybody tries to keep his back to the wall so no one can sneak
up behind and stab him. They're afraid of what may happen
next. The résumés from our management people looking for
new jobs are flying out of here as fast as the Xerox machines can grind."

"Uncertainty is a basic fact of life," said Hale. "Inse-
curity is the mother of invention. Pain is the spur."

"I believe you've got those aphorisms a little twisted."

"Perhaps the words, but not the sense," Hale said.
"Did you hear about the guy they warned not to smoke in
bed, that it would cost him his life someday? Well, sure
enough, he was smoking in bed one night and a man broke
into his room and killed him."

Fairweather laughed. "I guess beneath that heart of
stone you've got a cozy core of granite."

"Not really," Hale said softly. "I haven't always been
the cold, calculating businessman. Did you know I was a
concert violinist as a kid?"

"I guess I did read that in *Time* magazine."

"I gave recitals at Town Hall and I wrote poetry in Latin that won prizes. At Stuyvesant High I scored a 193 on the IQ test, the highest they ever saw there. But I could never play ball with the kids in the street. I never learned how to catch. Isn't that something? I could do Double-Crostics and the *Times* Sunday crossword puzzle when I was twelve. But I could never learn to catch a ball, any kind of ball. They'd laugh at me and I'd run up to my room and grab the violin and race through the 'Minute Waltz' in forty-five seconds. I was competitive as hell, but I had no outlet."

"Haight, you don't have to justify yourself to me. I admire your ability and I respect your judgment."

"But you despise me as a man."

"Not at all . . ."

"You're like all the rest. Envious. You're a plodder and you resent my success. The world is full of guys like you, putting one foot after the other. But you guys never make the breakthroughs. You have no imagination. And you haven't the nerve to take risks. Big risks for big profits."

"How did this turn into a personal attack on me?"

"I had my Ph.D. in comparative lit at twenty, and at twenty-three I already had made two million dollars in the market. My father was a railroad conductor who never made more than $141.50 a week in his life. Now he and my mother live like royalty in Phoenix, sunning their asses, telling themselves what a great job they did making such a smart son."

"You had the concert stage and the world of literature open to you," said Fairweather. "How did you happen to go into finance?"

"Just by reading the business pages in my spare time. I saw all that money being made and I realized that with money went power. Power to move things and change things and make things happen. Why should I entertain slobs or teach morons? Those things are subservient, secondary. I wanted to see if I could be *primary*. And I did. I hit on a couple of fast-rising stocks. Put all my father's and my uncle's money in them, and in two years I had a stake."

"Then came the fund you managed."

"Yes," said Hale, "but just *managing* money wasn't enough. That game was outguessing market psychology, and it was fun for a while. But the big challenge was building a company and running it. Creating an entity. I think I refined the quick takeover and the use of debt-financing beyond anybody. And you know what helped me do it? Two emotions. Two basic human drives which I learned to harness. Greed and the desire for revenge."

Hale dismounted his Exercycle and drew himself up to his full 5′ 4″ of height. "If you stop and think about it, in every company I've taken over there has been at least one disgruntled insider who has felt abused and underpaid. I almost never had to locate him. He located *me*. He told me where all the bodies were buried and helped sell my deal internally. His payoff was my getting rid of certain guys who ranked over him when we took over, and a little sweetening of his bankroll. I always obliged. I'm a man of my word."

"Aren't you afraid that same technique will be used on you someday?"

"Sure. We're kind of ripe for it right now. Except no one would even want us until we straighten out the mess."

"Haight, that's one thing I've always admired about you. You can be a miserable bastard, but you're straightforward about it."

"I've always thought I have the potential to be a modern folk hero. If only I could find a good PR man to get the press to write the right things. Instead of that jerk who keeps saying he doesn't care about the truth, merely the semblance of the truth. Why doesn't he get somebody to do a story on my *philosophy* instead of my financial record?"

"I remember when we took over the Grimbledon Air Control Company in Truesdale, Illinois," said Fairweather. "The first day you went out there you called all the employees together in the company cafeteria and I'll never forget those opening remarks. 'Good morning, ladies and gentlemen. My name is Haight Harvey Hale. I'm twenty-nine years old and a smashing financial success. You people have been suffering for years with a loser, but now all that is going to change. Together we are going to make Grimbledon Air Control rich and vibrant again.' They were prepared to hate you, but they broke into cheers."

"We sure stirred up old Truesdale after that, didn't we?" said Hale. "One guy there told me that before I came there Truesdale was the kind of place where on Tuesdays everybody went to Rotary and on Wednesdays an A&P truck pulled into town and they all would go over and watch it unload."

"I guess *you've* done most of the unloading in Truesdale these last few months," said Fairweather.

"If I could unload the whole damn *town* now I'd feel a lot better," Hale said. "I wish I'd never heard of Grimbledon. There's another beautiful tax loss carry-forward in search of a place to go. Like a lousy tapeworm, we've chopped it up in pieces, but the losses in each of the pieces keep regenerating."

"What we need now," said Fairweather, "is another Century Insurance Company. That was beautiful."

"Century. I dream of that every time the phone rings with another finder telling me of some great new deal ready to fall into our laps. Our debt-equity ratio is so high now I don't know how much longer we can go on paying out all this interest. But another Century Insurance could make us healthy again. When we took over that dead-ass outfit and found those overstuffed reserves it was like finding the keys to Fort Knox."

"You sure set the Street on its ear when you declared that $45 per share dividend. We had 87 percent of the company then and we got almost $180 million out of that maneuver. And the beautiful part was you left Century's fire-and-casualty division, even after that payout, with reserves that were well within the requirements of the law."

Hale nodded several times but the smile of self-appreciation turned quickly to a frown. "You know why *we* could do that and *their* management couldn't? We had nothing at stake there but the numbers. They were trapped in the pattern of their historic growth, the years and decades of conservative insurance practice. They were Establishment and they had to defend their proper ways of doing business. We were anti-Establishment. We could freewheel. So we milked it, and moved on to the next case. We were really riding high in those days."

"But what we never figured on was the disastrous effect that Nixon's tight money policy would have on us," said Fairweather.

"It's the damn Vietnam War," said Hale. "We're a casualty of the war. It's got the students acting crazy, the blacks going wild, and the unions shoving harder and harder. Inflation gets worse and worse no matter what Washington does because the country's pouring so much wealth down the Indochinese rat hole.

"So naturally our earnings begin to slip. But the drop in our stock price is way out of proportion. The damn funds dumping killed us. My buddies, the fund managers. Suddenly they all hate me because our compound growth rate has gone to hell. You'd think I'd defiled their mothers the way they talk about me now."

"And with HHH stock way down, the good-looking deals dry up for us," said Fairweather. "We haven't made a deal in six months. Nobody will touch our convertibles and we've run out of borrowing power."

"Well, there's no question we have only one direction to go," said Hale. "We've just about run out the string on the economizing bit. We can chop a few more expensive heads here and there, but there's not much more we can squeeze out without mortally wounding the parts. We must start divesting, piece by piece, hoping things will turn around in the economy before we've cannibalized the company beyond redemption. Meanwhile, the funds we pick up on the divestitures will keep us out of the clutches of the banks."

"I'm afraid you're right, Haight," said Fairweather. "But this is an awful tough market to be forced to sell into. We'll take big capital losses on every division we sell, and that will knock our book value way down."

"To hell with book value," Hale said. "This is survival I'm talking about. The kind of cash squeeze we're in can put us out of the ball game in months."

"I agree."

"Listen. We've got to make this all seem planned and orderly or the vultures downtown will sell us down to nothing."

"How can we do that?"

"Well, let's put out a think piece to stockholders after our first divestiture," said Hale. "Let's have our public relations people work up something on our new policy of corporate purification. Let's say we have reexamined and clarified our mission and a new tighter ship will result."

"That sounds convincing."

"It better be, or I may have to start practicing that fiddle again," Hale said.

Just then Hale's pretty young secretary entered the room. "He's here," she said, smothering a giggle.

"I know," Hale said. "I can smell him through the walls. It's his new all-purpose cologne and pubic spray called Prince's Passion. I'm surprised you're still on your feet, dear."

As the secretary left to usher in the prince, Hale turned to Fairweather and said, "Act I, Scene I of new drama about to start. Will youthful corporate empire builder succeed in new role of disconglomerator? Or will the blood merely flow on all he touches? Tune in again this time next year and see if he's still around."

13 / The Snake Pit

WHEN TIGHT MONEY MAKES CASH TENDER OFFERS VIRTU-
ally impossible, as in early 1970, and when the severely
depressed stock prices and price-earnings ratios of many
hitherto swinging conglomerate companies sharply restrict
their ability to make attractive paper offers, the old-fashioned proxy contest comes back in style as the least difficult
way to take over a vulnerable company.

"Least difficult" is used advisedly. Proxy fights are almost never easy; they tend to be long, sordid, soul-
wrenching, and very expensive. What's more, a contesting
group can lose even though it seems objectively to have
right and justice on its side. Nor does careful planning and
tactical skill guarantee success; at the very last minute, an
intransigent Justice Department or federal regulatory
agency can convert victory into defeat. Proxy fights can be
lost for any number of reasons, many not even barely relating to the issues in contention. Yet they are once again increasing in frequency, and more than one battle-scarred veteran foresees a rash of new wars developing.

To many who were close to the company, the wonder
was that Basic International Foodstuffs, Inc. had managed
to stay out of the clutches of a raider even this long. Its un-
imaginative, ultraconservative management had steered it
away from every growth opportunity in the grocery business
for the last twenty years, while paying off all its debts and
hoarding its surplus cash. If the management had set out to
construct a perfect lure it could hardly have done a better
job. So it came as no great surprise to the Street when

Ephraim Rader announced his substantial holdings in BIF and indicated his intention to seek to bring about a merger of BIF with his company.

Among the genus "conglomerator," Rader was considered one of the best. He was a business organization expert in addition to being a financial whiz, having spent a number of years with such management consulting firms as McKinsey and Cresap, McCormick and Paget before striking out on his own. In the course of building his own company to its present eminence he took over and rejuvenated several major companies, including a moribund railroad, an over-asseted paper and carton manufacturer, and a dying meat-packer along with a spray of diverse smaller operations in commercial solvents, cigars, brassieres and girdles, auto rentals, building materials, Little League uniforms, and neopornographic literature. In each case the acquired company's balance sheet greatly benefited from his ministrations, though many of the people therein did not get to hang around long enough to witness the completion of the miracle. But Rader had always captured his prey through a cash or stock tender offer when a "friendly" merger could not be worked out. Each conquest was speedy and therefore relatively inexpensive; gaining his objective with blitzkrieg attacks, he then used the victim's assets to finance his deals. The current action was the first time he found it necessary to engage in a full-fledged proxy fight.

As always, he went about the job with characteristic thoroughness. He secured an accurate analysis of the many mistakes of BIF's management over the last several years. He lined up some powerful Wall Street investment banking firms to act as dealer-managers to help him gather stock and attract fund votes. He nominated the best of his own company's directors along with a few outside celebrities as the contending slate in the proxy contest. And he retained shrewd and experienced legal, proxy soliciting, and public relations counsel to work as a team with him and his chief financial aides.

The Rader build-up program started months before the announcement of his holdings in BIF. With conglomerates having generally fallen to low esteem, his public relations people concentrated on showing Rader as a careful assets manager and his company, Inter-American Industries, as a unique multioperational firm that developed a high degree of synergism among its parts in contrast to the wild heterogeneous melange that characterized the average conglomerate. An article in *Investor's Reader* admiringly traced the entire history of Rader's acquisition program, and a story in *Financial World* spotlighted the "jewel of the conglomerates" and recommended it as an interesting speculation. *Dun's Review* profiled Rader as a man on the move once again.

Meanwhile Rader visited Kansas City, BIF's headquarters city, and managed to be seen about town with some of the most important businessmen and politicians, be interviewed extensively on local radio and television, and be quoted on a variety of subjects in the local newspapers. Rader's purpose: ingratiate himself in BIF's own backyard to try to short-circuit any possible local crusade against his taking over the big local industry that could lead to troublesome legislation or congressional harassment.

Rader and his communications specialists had done all this sort of thing before, so they merely rewarmed the successful recipe and sprinkled in a little spice of local issues, Kansas City style. As luck would have it, the BIF management did not have very good community or press relations because of their long-standing tradition of noncooperation whenever possible. Thus Rader's efforts were doubly effective, thanks to BIF's residual ill will.

In the face of this smoothly running Rader juggernaut, the BIF strategy team began to gird itself for a rough proxy battle. Executive vice president Richard Anderson's thrown-down gauntlet earned him the presidency many months ahead of schedule, and he set foot in office, running. He made several quick internal moves to cut personnel costs, consolidate manufacturing, and reposition the company in its strongest product fields. The new convertible preferred issue was placed successfully with friendly foreign interests (at the cost of several franchise concessions in addition to a bargain price), thereby adding to the votes that management could count on.

Still, the depressed price of BIF stock after two years of declining earnings and a reduced dividend was hard to explain away. The only course seemed to be to place the blame squarely at the feet of recently resigned top management. Anderson saw with painful clarity that it was that or

an abortive end to his chief executive career. To emphasize his break with the past he started systematically terminating all but three corporate vice presidents. Within a month he had a new first-line team, had consolidated and thereby eliminated four of the company's nine divisions, had dropped three major product lines, and had severed 3,000 of the company's 24,000 employees.

Then Anderson wrote a letter to all 32,000 BIF stockholders detailing his actions and explaining how his over-all modernization program would bring BIF once again to the top of its industry. He placed full page ads in the financial pages of newspapers in twelve leading cities to impress this message on investment community leaders as well. There was still some hope that all this show of aggressive action might head off Rader's proxy attack by making him question his chances of winning. But Rader had gone too far down the road to turn back now. The issue was joined a few days later when Rader came out of SEC registration and shot his opening salvo through an interview in the *New York Times* in which he averred he planned to dethrone BIF management for irresponsible and inept handling of stockholders' assets. He indicated that Anderson and the new group around him were simply younger versions of the old president and chairman who had so criminally mismanaged the company. As a major stockholder, Rader said that he was naturally very concerned about his investment, and that he had offered to take over the management of the company, only to be rudely rejected.

An emergency council of war was called by Anderson for that very evening. The meeting was held again in the New York law office of Hendricks, Stuffwell & Longdale, and present were Anderson and three of his BIF aides; Stuart LaCroix of the House of Vehl, BIF's main invest-

ment banker; Manny Oxenberg, the proxy lawyer; Jim
Robbe, the proxy solicitor; Frank Quigley, the PR counselor; and Clarence Stuffwell and a clutch of his acolytes. In
short, the strategic high command.

The first task they assigned themselves as a group was
to try to estimate the likely lineup of votes if the proxy contest were to take place tomorrow. There were 12,750,000
common shares outstanding and 250,000 convertible preferred with five votes per share, or a total of 14,000,000
votes. BIF management could count on 1,250,000 votes
from the friendly foreign-held preferred that was recently
placed, and 400,000 votes from the holdings of all the current directors and officers, or a total of 1,650,000.

Rader owned a known 2.1 million with perhaps another few hundred thousand held by people associated
with him. That left more than 10,000,000 of the
14,000,000 votes not definitely committed as of the moment. In round figures the noncommitted stock broke down
as follows:

Three million held by various mutual funds and trusts,
a figure that had increased ominously from 2,000,000 in recent months indicating some of the go-go boys might be
looking for some artificial price action; 2,000,000 held by
bank trust departments; 2,200,000 held by brokerage
houses in various Street names; 3,000,000 held by some
30,000 individual stockholders around the country, with
heaviest concentrations in New York, Missouri (BIF's
headquarters state), California, and Florida (the big retire-
ment states where the widows go to live on their pensions
and dividends).

The BIF strategists decided that most of the fund stock
would probably go for Rader's slate because he had many
friends among the fund managers, who had made a lot of
money betting on him in the past. On the other hand, most

of the bank-held stock should stick with BIF now that new management had taken over. The banks hardly ever go for the raider, especially against an Establishment-type company. And now that a specific, positive program for improving profits was in being at BIF, they had a good enough fiduciary reason to help justify their natural sentiments.

Nothing was to be taken for granted, of course. House of Vehl people, along with Anderson and Mike Caldwell, BIF's new young financial vice president who was brought in from a hot conglomerate, would call on all the leading fund managers who owned BIF stock as well as the bank trust officers. But they did not expect any surprises.

Thus preliminary estimates by the strategists gave Rader 5,100,000 votes (his owned stock plus fund stock) to 3,650,000 for BIF management (the friendly foreign interests plus stock owned by company directors and officers), with approximately 7,000,000 needed for certain victory. Therefore the 2,200,000 shares held by the brokers and the 3,000,000 owned by the individual stockholders held the key to the contest.

One ace in the hole yet to be played by BIF management was the acquisition of a privately held packaging company for one million shares of BIF authorized but unissued common. This deal had been in the lukewarm negotiation stage for months. The price had been considered too high under ordinary circumstances, but circumstances currently were far from ordinary.

At the strategy meeting, the decision was made to go ahead with the EZ Open deal and give the million shares. Although EZ Open was not worth it, the big block of BIF stock given in payment would have the special virtue of nicely supplementing management's proxy tally. BIF's 14,000,000 outstanding shares would become 15,000,000 with the additional stock issued, and BIF management could then count on 4,650,000 vs. Rader's 5,100,000. Because it is axiomatic that at least 10 percent of the stock will never get voted in any proxy contest, that meant Rader would need approximately 1,700,000 of the broker and individual stockholder total of 5,250,000 while BIF management would need around 2,100,000 in order to get the kind of vote needed to win.

With the purchase decision made, assignments were given out by Anderson to Burnham, the corporate secretary, and to young Caldwell. Stuffwell commented on the likelihood of a lawsuit by Rader, but Oxenberg, the proxy law specialist, assured the group that no court would rule against BIF management, for they were well within their rights as stated in the New York Stock Exchange regulations. Then the grand planners turned to the subject of how to get those crucial 2,100,000 additional votes.

"Rader will probably pick up a few hundred thousand proxies by getting some friends to buy on the market," Oxenberg said. "He may also squeeze a little more cash out of his own company to buy some, but there isn't too much cash left there. He's got to get most of his minimum of one million seven the way we'll have to get our two million one. Piece by piece, the hard way."

"When is the annual meeting scheduled?" asked Robbe, the proxy soliciting expert.

"April 29," said Burnham.

"That's very bad," said Robbe. "There'll be two thousand or more annual meetings that week in April—it's the heaviest time of the year. The brokers' back offices will be swamped. Since we'll need 50 percent more votes out of the brokers than Rader will, we'll be more hurt than him by their inability to move the proxies out."

"Even if you pay off the back-office clerks?" said Waldo Craven, Clarence Stuffwell's ace assistant. Craven tried to emphasize his cleverness with a knowing leer.

"The point is," Robbe said, "that their *normal* operations are so screwed up down there that in late April it'll be like Hiroshima after the bomb. Between that and the crazy mail service, I think we'll be in big trouble. I'll get a trickle out, but we need a stream."

"What if we move the annual meeting back a month to late May?" said Oxenberg. "That will take it out of the busiest time. But it will also make for a much longer solicitation period. Will that help us or hurt us?"

"That means much greater costs to us," said Burnham, the corporate secretary.

"That's *your* decision," said Robbe. "But the extra time could help us in the soliciting out in the boondocks. It will give our new management story a better chance to sink in. We'll be able to get Dick Anderson better known and around to see more people. And we might even have some good news to report by then to show new management's effectiveness."

"Whether we spend $500,000 or $1,000,000," said Anderson calmly, "we have to view this as total war. We have to believe that what we are doing is best for the BIF stockholders or we wouldn't all be here tonight. So we should spend whatever is necessary to do this thing right. I'm sure as hell not interested in coming in second."

Some pretty sanctimonious reasoning there, thought Quigley. Stockholder interests are not necessarily synonomous with Anderson interests and opposite to Rader interests. Yet, though Quigley privately believed the whole business of attack, defense, and counterattack as practiced at the highest levels in hundreds of boardrooms all over the country to be economically wasteful and destructive, he rather admired the way Anderson handled himself. With a business background of grocery marketing and general sales administration, Anderson suddenly found himself forced to make crucial decisions in an arena totally foreign to him. Thrust into the position of fighting for his business life he was clawing and scheming as hard as he could. But he does it with a touch of class, thought Quigley. And his people seem to believe in him.

It was decided unanimously that the annual meeting would be officially set for May 20 at the next regular BIF board meeting next week. The annual reports to stockholders would be mailed in early March with proxies enclosed.

Then the question of the stockholder mailing lists was taken up. Rader had already officially requested the list.

"Must we give it to him?" asked Burnham.

"If we don't he'll take us to court and get the list in five or six days anyway," said Oxenberg. "We're a Delaware corporation and Delaware law says he is entitled to see the lists if he has a proper purpose, and a proxy solicitation for a rival slate of directors is a proper purpose. However, it is nowhere stated that we have to furnish him with neat computerized tapes. We only have to make the lists available to him. If you have them on individual cards for example, you can let him come in and copy off all 32,000 names. Meanwhile we should be getting our first mailing out to the stockholders. And that first mailing is very important."

"It certainly is," said Stuffwell, anxious to exhibit some of his high-priced expertise. After all, this was *his* paneled boardroom. He ought to have *some* important things to say. "Many stockholders read the first proxy, sign it, and never look at any of the subsequent ones."

"We've got to get our best positive story into that first letter," said Quigley. "We should also put that letter into a financial page ad again."

"The last ad we placed got excellent reaction from our distributors and retailers," said Anderson. "They think we're showing new vigor and determination."

"We'll be getting out four or five letters with proxies before the May 20 annual meeting," said Oxenberg, lighting a meditative cigar at the same time. "And so will Rader. Many BIF stockholders will get so confused they won't know what to do. It is important, therefore, that we have a short powerful wrap-up letter to the stockholders timed to be the last piece of mail they receive, with just enough time for them to do something with it before the annual meeting. While I'm sure by then the stockholders will be sick and tired of both sides, the fact is that there is a fair percentage of automatic signers who are just the opposite of the one-look-and-that's-all type that Mr. Stuffwell mentioned. These automatic signers sign everything, usually for both sides. That's why it is important that we get in the last mailing as well as the first. Because, as you know, the last dated proxy invalidates all the others that have preceded it from that stockholder."

"For psychological effect," said Quigley, "we might even have the reply envelope of the last mailing bear tongue-licked stamps. Some people can't bear to see real, stamped envelopes go to waste, and they mail in the proxy, invalidating everything they sent in before. But since all that stamp-licking and pasting will take a fair amount of time, we ought to get started on that special set of envelopes as soon as possible and then lock them away."

The actual stockholder solicitation was the next item on the agenda. Here Robbe, the man of the people, came onto center stage. He suggested that all stockholders with holdings of 500 or more shares be contacted personally by an officer of BIF with a prepared set of points to be made. This kind of attention is flattering to the stockholder and can often swing him over into the management column. The smaller stockholders, numbering perhaps 25,000, would be contacted by phone by Robbe's network of professional solicitors all over the country. Robbe and his chief lieutenants would work on the brokers' proxy clerks while the top BIF financial people and the Vehl partners contacted the brokerage house partners to try to get orders for special handling for BIF proxies passed down to the back office personnel.

Supplementing all this, and reinforcing it considerably, was a suggestion made by Oxenberg. He told Anderson that the BIF sales organization could be put to use quite effectively. Scores of district sales managers, branch managers, and just ordinary salesmen could personally call on stockholders in their territories and plead for their votes. They could tell how all this turmoil caused by Rader was hurting the company and, even worse, what dire things might happen to them and their wives and small children if Rader should win. They should even have pictures with their clean, nonhippie looking kids and dogs to show.

"Jim Robbe is an artist at putting that kind of tearjerking story together for your men," said Oxenberg. "It was just that kind of doorbell-ringing campaign that saved the day for Occidental Plaster & Wallboard against Hiram Wolfe last year. We thought we were dead on that one for sure until the Aunt Janes were touched and turned their tears into votes."

Robbe smiled in recollection and agreed to help put together a proper East Lynne script for BIF's minions to rend hearts around the country, while Quigley wondered what would happen to the grocery sales with all the salesmen out soliciting proxies.

The meeting lasted well past midnight. When it broke up, everybody knew his assignment and the defensive machine was primed to go on the offensive. Anderson and his BIF aides got into Stuffwell's waiting limousine and were driven to the airport where their private jet was standing by to whisk them back to Kansas City in time to catch three hours sleep before they started the next business day.

That was the pace at which all the principals in the BIF defense command traveled during the next two months. Anderson's schedule was truly backbreaking. He shuttled from office to plants all over the country, feverishly trying to cut costs and build sales. His goal was to turn the earnings curve around quickly so that he could report a successful first quarter before the annual meeting vote of the stockholders. He also called on major stockholders wherever they lived to ask for their vote of confidence in him and his new team, as well as on leading fund managers in Boston and Chicago, and key bankers in New York and San Francisco. Somehow, he also found time for periodic meetings with his proxy advisers in New York to check on the progress of the war.

The votes from the small stockholders were coming in well but predictably the brokers' proxies were almost nonexistent while the fund managers were cold and the bankers encouraging. After every proxy-soliciting letter went out, Robbe's professional solicitors in the field tested the appeal of each argument in the letter and let the command post in New York know which seemed most effective and which seemed least effective with stockholders. They also reported which parts of Rader's appeals were scoring and needed to be countered by BIF management. Sometimes Rader's points could not be refuted directly, so the only thing to do was attack him on another front. A dossier on Rader's weaknesses, ones that might be converted into mortal blemishes casting doubt on his character and business judgment, was hastily gathered for that purpose.

It came down to the last few days before the annual meeting with the tentative vote lineup, judging from the proxies already in, beginning to look so close that the swing of one big block could decide it all. Each side sent out final letters with their strongest arguments simply and clearly restated in terms of the individual stockholder's self-interest. These letters arrived in the same mail in 32,000 mailboxes around the country.

With control of one of the world's largest food manufacturing companies hanging in the balance, the spotlight shifted to the counting room. Or, as it is known among veteran proxy fighters, the snake pit. Here the denouement to this high corporate drama was to be resolved. It was in a second-floor room in the Muelbach Hotel in Kansas City. The BIF annual meeting was held in the hotel's ballroom, and after the business of the meeting was completed on May 20, the meeting was adjourned to permit the inspectors of election to tabulate the proxies.

Three mutually agreed-upon independent inspectors of election were there, but the principal actors on the scene were Manny Oxenberg, representing Basic International Foodstuffs, and his counterpart lawyer, Will Otis, representing Ephraim Rader and Inter-American Industries.

In a contest as close as this one with 32,000 stockholders of record each solicited ten or more times and an aggregate of 120,000 proxies (including duplicates) to be hand counted, the snake pit could last several weeks, with some twenty to thirty auditors assisting the inspectors milling around among the tables piled with proxy cards, envelopes, coffee containers, and sandwich wrappers under a pall of stale blue smoke. Hardly a heroic setting for such a major event.

Oxenberg and Otis, with the acquiescence of their clients, agreed to a "short count" method to facilitate the tabulation. Under this arrangement, the parties turn over all proxies and envelopes to the inspectors, who are allowed to make a dry run without interference by either side. Both Oxenberg and Otis had been through the grueling counting procedure many times before, and they knew that a "long count" with representatives for each side along with the inspectors sitting at tables and jointly examining and perhaps challenging 120,000 proxies could take many weeks or even months.

As it was it took more than a week for the inspectors to complete their dry run on the BIF proxies and give their tentative unofficial figures to both sides. Following this, each side was given an opportunity to inspect the winning proxies of the other side and to raise questions or challenge tentative rulings. That took another few days. The most common challenges came on the matter of dates on proxies. Almost all were eventually resolved one way or another, some by the dates on the envelopes in which they were received. Questionable signatures—those that did not conform with corporate records or seemed possible forgeries—temporarily negated another batch of votes. A few proxies were thrown out when one side proved the stockholder was actually dead at the time of the voting, and still others for such "technicalities" as the stockholder being an infant or a proven incompetent lacking the power to vote or give proxies.

A total of 13,321,833 valid proxies were cast, out of a possible 15,061,721, for an unusually high 89 percent vote. When all the challenged proxies by both sides were balanced out, it seemed evident that the BIF slate of directors had managed to squeak in by a tally of 6,850,000 to 6,500,000.

The winning difference appeared to be in the unusually heavy vote of the small stockholders. Despite BIF's poor financial record and bad stock price action, the over-whelming majority of individual stockholders seemed willing to accept the story of BIF's new management team and to let them try to pull the company out of its doldrums.

In retrospect, the long solicitation campaign to scrape the votes out of the woodwork probably was the key piece of strategy. But the individual stockholders undoubtedly were predisposed in favor of management anyway; many of the more disgruntled individuals already had sold their stock (which subsequently showed up in the funds' column where it was voted in favor of Rader).

Of course, the clear-cut victory would not be recorded for months because of formal challenges to some of the proxies in court and Rader's still unresolved suit against management for buying EZ Open Company with one million shares of BIF treasury stock "to the detriment of BIF stockholders as a class."

But Rader himself knew he had been beaten. He was faced now with the choice of selling his BIF stock at a multimillion dollar loss to go with the substantial costs of the lost proxy fight and the sizable interest carrying charges, or holding the big block and paying continuing interest charges and tying up all that capital for another year while waiting for Anderson to fall on his face so that a proxy fight might succeed at the next annual meeting. Whatever choice he made, he knew ultimately he would have to answer to his own stockholders. He had never really had to think about that before.

14 / Thunder from the East

THE DOW JONES BROAD TAPE CLATTERED OUT THE SAD news: Dawson Communications' earnings for the year had plummeted from $3.10 per share to 28 cents, the fourth quarter was in the red, and the board of directors had voted to omit the quarterly dividend.

In a matter of minutes trading in Dawson stock was suspended on the floor of the New York Stock Exchange as the specialist gasped for air under an avalanche of sell orders. Three hours and many excited conferences with Exchange officials later, the ashen-faced specialist was able to muster his resources and absorb enough stock to maintain a market and reopen trading in the Dawson stock at 16, down 9 from the last previous sale.

The stock rallied a bit from that point, but sank again under another selling wave by the end of the day to a low of 13½. (Only three months before it had been at 62, and a year ago, 114. Dawson's peak, two years previously, had been 121.)

After the close, two of the specialist's partners helped carry him back to his office. "If only my hippie son could see me now," he said piteously. "The frontier is *here*. Africa, shmafrica, I need my own personal Peace Corps. They're assassinating me out there."

But in a boardroom somewhere in southern Tokyo, some help for the specialist was about to start on its way. Noting the ten-year low just recorded by Dawson Communications, the directors of Mitsushandi, the huge Japanese conglomerate, muttered the business equivalent of "banzai" as the decision was made to begin buying Dawson common again the next day. Two years ago they had bought a few thousand shares through various Swiss and American representatives, but a rising market put Dawson stock up too high for them to accumulate an appreciable amount. Now with a new, more relaxed Japanese regulation permitting Japanese companies to buy up to $100 million of foreign securities, and with the American stock market and Dawson stock way down, they resolved not to stop short of absolute control.

And so the next day a tentative firmness in Dawson developed right at the opening bell. The specialist, already overly fortified with tranquilizers in anticipation of another black day, was grateful. But around midday one of his partners pointed out the curiously persistent nature of the demand that had developed. The stock closed up 2 for the day on good steady volume.

The demand continued for three more days, driving the stock up seven points on rising volume, then suddenly stopped. The specialist grew concerned again and had to drop the price four points before he could find another buyer.

That was the pattern for five weeks. Just when the specialist expected volume to regularize, it stopped completely and he was forced to drop the price back. Then demand would pick up again from a new source. At the end of the five-week period, the net advance was six points from the bottom to 13½ to 19½. The specialist suspected someone was toying with him, but he could not be sure because at least eight houses had been doing the buying. He was quite annoyed, however, that he was not able to get more of his money back on the upside even though the five-week trading volume totaled 1,250,000—seven times the company's customary volume.

Meanwhile at Dawson corporate headquarters in Denver, the financial vice president and the executive vice president had grown sufficiently alarmed to consider discussing their concern with Henry Carroll Dawson, the sixty-seven-year-old founder, chief stockholder, chairman of the board, and president of the firm.

"I think it's finally happening," said the financial vice president. "Somebody ought to tell the old man."

"Who?" said the executive vice president.

"I guess you should—you're the next highest ranking officer."

"He won't believe it. Anyway, he won't want to hear about it and he'll never forgive me for bringing it up."

"But we've got to do *something*."

"Let's hire a consultant to tell him," said the executive vice president. "He can fire the consultant, but maybe the idea will get through to him."

"Good thought. Who should we hire?"

"I don't know. Why don't you ask our law firm?"

"Not me. I don't want the old man learning it was my idea to hire a consulting firm he had to fire because of their crazy ideas. You know how long I'd last then."

"Okay. It's a job for the corporate secretary anyway. I'll ask Rogers to do it."

Henry Carroll Dawson ruled his company as firmly as he had forty-two years ago when he started it in a room over the garage of his parents' home in Boulder, Colorado. He was then a young Ph.D., just out of the University of Wisconsin. He had already a half-dozen electronic patents to his credit, and had hand-built some of the finest radio receivers in the West. His younger brother, Willard, joined him and became the businessman of the new organization. Henry concentrated on inventing. From radios he moved on to high quality recording equipment and then television tubes. During World War II he did much of the pioneering

work on radar, and invented several electronic mine detectors and sniper detectors which helped American armies limit their casualties as they swept the Japanese across the Pacific. Ironically, twenty-five years later the Japanese were to sweep back to capture Henry Carroll Dawson.

After the war, Dawson Communications was the armed forces' leading supplier of electronic detecting and communications equipment. By the early fifties it had grown to a $100 million a year business with a reputation for top quality work. The Denver plant was enlarged and a new one was built in Seattle. Henry Carroll Dawson by then had over two hundred varied patents in his own name and was regarded by some as perhaps the most original mind in electronic communications since Marconi.

Then, in 1955, Willard Dawson, the vice chairman and business brain of the company, the man who had engineered its move from the Boulder garage proprietorship to a major publicly owned downtown Denver corporation, was killed in a skiing accident in Aspen. Since he could trust no one the way he had trusted his younger brother, Henry Dawson, after a brief period of mourning, took on the business responsibilities in addition to the technical and production duties of the company.

By now the company was leading the way in sophisticated missile and rocket guidance systems. It employed more than 3,000 scientists and engineers. Indeed it was said that it had more Ph.D.'s on its payroll than all but two companies in the United States. Dawson Communications gradually branched out into the manufacture of a variety of precision electronic equipment. Almost invariably the pattern was the same: Henry Dawson and his engineers decided certain parts they had to buy on the market were not of sufficiently high quality so they resolved to make the parts themselves. Semiconductors, multiple printed circuit boards, and many delicate measuring devices were carefully and expensively manufactured at the Denver or Seattle plants. A few industrial company purchasing agents learned of this precision manufacturing capability and went to Dawson for specialized parts, willingly paying the considerably higher prices. Slowly, among certain industrial *cognoscenti,* Dawson developed a reputation for tops in quality of product, though noncompetitive on a mass basis.

But in Wall Street the image of the company settled into an unflattering mold: defense contractor. Its price-to-earnings multiple moved in the boom and bust pattern of that group. Thus two years ago when Dawson's earnings per share rose to $6.94 the price of the stock peaked at only 121, or slightly more than seventeen times earnings, while some of the glamour stocks were selling at fifty or sixty times or higher.

The Street, however, was not well-informed about Dawson. True, 50 percent of its $380 million volume last year came from government agencies; yet more than half the government's purchases were off-the-shelf hardware rather than special contract work (which the investment community regards nervously because there is always the danger of short notice cancellation or cutback). One frustrated security analyst, who was heavily committed in the stock, commented that Dawson Communications told its story to the Street with greater ineptitude than any company in his memory. Henry Carroll Dawson himself was considered something of a mystery man; at best a legendary genius, at worst a weird nonbusiness-oriented scientific nut. Only once in his life had Henry Dawson ever visited New York City. That was six years ago at the insistence of his lead bank, which was arranging a $100 million loan. He came into town late one night in his private jet, stayed through lunch the next day to meet with the bank's executive committee, and was in the air winging back to Denver by 3:00 P.M. One bank vice president who helped escort him through most of the truncated day counted a total of twenty-three words spoken by him, in addition to three hellos and good-byes.

Science, of course, was Dawson's Holy Grail. Projected fiscal plans and budgets were like so many child's doodlings to Henry Dawson. The quest for knowledge— that was what interested him. The annual research and development budget at Dawson Communications was the highest as a percent of sales of any company listed on the New York Stock Exchange. But if Henry Dawson and his cohorts were on the trail of something he considered important, and the monetary allowance ran out, he would merely amble into the treasurer's office and say, "Michael, we're going to need another two million to finish the transverse photoconductive widget project."

"But Mr. Dawson, we're already over budget and the three-year plan is in danger."

"We must get this right. The new data system depends on it."

It was a cliché in the company that Henry Dawson always did what he wanted. He had a whim of iron, and plans and budgets were built around his personal desires. This was suspected, too, by some of the more sophisticated money managers and analysts, and Dawson stock was thereby down-graded as an investment.

For the last three years, the one project that absorbed Henry Dawson's total dedication was the new Dawson computer. This was a small, highly efficient, and complex computer built to undersell anything IBM had on the market. It was capable of talking to other computers, operating factories, running trains, and flying airplanes. It was a new generation in computerdom. Medical diagnoses, military campaign plans, and long-range weather prediction were all within its power. Henry Dawson himself invented several of the important components. Most of the manufacturing operations at the two big Dawson Communications plants and two satellite plants were already being run by the new Dawson data control system. The company had a research investment of $80 million in this system, and it was now ready to start selling it to industry.

Actually it had been ready for several months. Henry Dawson had put the word out about it discreetly, expecting his doors to be hammered down by companies swarming to buy his better mousetrap. But it had not happened. Somehow industry did not regard Dawson Communications as the fountain of knowledge in the computer field. This disappointed Henry Dawson intensely. He was finally prevailed upon by some of his associates to advertise this marvelous new data system. He agreed, but when the copy for the ads was submitted to him, he found it inaccurate. He spent three days and nights rewriting and revising it before he allowed it to run. By then the copy was almost unintelligible to anyone but an advanced mathematician. Hardly any company presidents—who, after all, are the men who make the decisions to buy new computer systems—could get past the first paragraph.

Not a single Dawson system was sold, although the Dawson financial vice president was projecting computer sales to be one-third of the company's over-all business in three years. Meanwhile, production stretch-outs and outright cancellations in big government agency technological projects, combined with tight money conditions which caused much postponing of capital purchases by industry, hit Dawson's over-all sales hard and affected its earnings picture severely. Still Henry Dawson refused to cut down his research expenditures, much of which continued to be channeled into the perfecting of the new computer system, which he saw as the crowning scientific achievement of his life.

The stock of the company started to drop as if in a chute. With each quarterly announcement of further declining earnings it plunged still farther. It made the trip from 114 to 13½ in less than a year. Hardly any quality company could match that record. With 3,500,000 shares outstanding, the company's total valuation in the market dropped in that short time from nearly $400 million to less than $50 million. Henry Dawson's substantial holding of 600,000 shares dropped in value from almost $70 million to just over $8 million. But he hardly realized it. Money was a commodity he barely understood. He had not carried money on his person to pay for anything for years. He never got involved with income taxes or personal expenses. He had not the faintest idea, for instance, of the cost of a suit of clothes or a tankful of gasoline or a meal in a restaurant. Aides, advisers, and servants had shielded him from all that vulgarity for years. The quest for truth was his single-minded drive. Henry Carroll Dawson was an eighteenth-century scientific lord heading a publicly owned twentieth-century corporation. Henry Dawson believed it was his company to run as he chose—but he owned only one-sixth of it.

The leaders of Mitsushandi were perfectly aware of that. Their investigators had settled on Dawson Communications as the best way for them to leap into the forefront of computer technology. Japan has trailed the United States abjectly in this vital industry, which may soon be the biggest in the world. Here was a gold mine in advanced electronic technology that could be bought for a fraction of its true worth. When the agents for Mitsushandi started buying Dawson common stock the total market valuation on the company was just about $50 million. Although they knew the price would go up as they dried up the available stock float, they expected to be able to get at least 51 percent for approximately $35 million. They actually accomplished it under budget.

They wanted 1,750,000-plus shares. They started with several thousand shares previously owned. Most of the rest was picked up in small blocks over the five-week period after the bad news of the most recent earnings drop and omitted dividend. A few larger blocks were bought off-the-market from funds eager to unload.

Then one windless, sunny day in Denver, two Japanese neatly dressed in dark blue business suits appeared in the reception room of the Dawson Communications Company.

"We would be honored to have the pleasure of meeting with Mr. Henry Carroll Dawson," one of them told the receptionist. "We represent the Mitsushandi Company of Tokyo."

"Do you have an appointment?"

"No, Miss. We have just flown in from Tokyo."

"I'm afraid Mr. Dawson does not see anybody except by appointment."

"Please, Miss. Inform him we would like very much to see him. Our company now owns controlling interest in this company."

"Well, I'll tell his secretary. But I'm sure that won't make any difference."

The two Japanese looked quizzically at each other. Had something been omitted from their instructions?

After several minutes, a gaunt gray-haired man of medium height, wearing a short-sleeved white shirt with a dark green tie, strode through a door into the reception room and came over to the two Japanese and said he was Henry Carroll Dawson and asked what they wanted.

"We have urgent business to discuss with you. Our company, Mitsushandi of Tokyo, now owns 55 percent of Dawson Communications."

"So?"

"We would like to meet with you in private. We have certain messages from our head office for you, and certain programs we have been instructed to discuss with you."

"I'm too busy for that sort of thing right now. In the middle of a sensitive experiment. Please come back some other day."

The two Japanese businessmen looked at each other in amazement. Then one said to the other, in Japanese, "Is he crazy?"

The other shrugged. "Who can tell with these inscrutable Occidentals?"

Epilogue

THE NICE THING ABOUT LIFE ON THE MERGER FRONT IS that so many new and fascinating things are always happening. It may indeed be our last frontier, the place where boldness and initiative are rewarded beyond all else.

For the fainthearted or irresolute, however, it can be the nearest thing to hell. They are the pigeons, and for each of them there is a predator. And the big daily scoreboard registers the course of the action in eighths and quarters.

Someone once said that winning isn't everything, but it sure beats whatever comes in second. Trouble is, what happens after winning?